The History of Classical Music

The History of Classical Music

Stuart A. Kallen

LUCENT BOOKS

A part of Gale, Cengage Learning

GALE
CENGAGE Learning

Detroit • New York • San Francisco • New Haven, Conn • Waterville, Maine • London

LIBRARY OF CONGRESS CATALOGING-IN-PUBLICATION DATA

Kallen, Stuart A., 1955-
 The history of classical music / by Stuart A. Kallen.
   pages cm. -- (The music library)
 Includes bibliographical references and index.
 ISBN 978-1-4205-0944-1 (hardcover)
 1. Music--History and criticism--Juvenile literature. I. Title.
 ML3928.K35 2013
 781.6809--dc23
                                      2012046028

Lucent Books
27500 Drake Rd
Farmington Hills MI 48331

ISBN-13: 978-1-4205-0944-1
ISBN-10: 1-4205-0944-6

Printed in the United States of America
1 2 3 4 5 6 7 17 16 15 14 13

CONTENTS

In the nineteenth century, English novelist Charles Kingsley wrote, "Music speaks straight to our hearts and spirits, to the very core and root of our souls. . . . Music soothes us, stirs us up . . . melts us to tears." As Kingsley stated, music is much more than just a pleasant arrangement of sounds. It is the resonance of emotion, a joyful noise, a human endeavor that can soothe the spirit or excite the soul. Musicians can also imitate the expressive palette of the earth, from the violent fury of a hurricane to the gentle flow of a babbling brook.

The word *music* is derived from the fabled Greek muses, the children of Apollo who ruled the realms of inspiration and imagination. Composers have long called upon the muses for help and insight. Music is not merely the result of emotions and pleasurable sensations, however.

Music is a discipline subject to formal study and analysis. It involves the juxtaposition of creative elements such as rhythm, melody, and harmony with intellectual aspects of composition, theory, and instrumentation. Like painters mixing red, blue, and yellow into thousands of colors, musicians blend these various elements to create classical symphonies, jazz improvisations, country ballads, and rock-and-roll tunes.

Throughout centuries of musical history, individual musical elements have been blended and modified in infinite ways. The resulting sounds may convey a whole range of moods, emotions, reactions, and messages. Music, then, is both an expression and reflection of human experience and emotion.

The foundations of modern musical styles were laid down by the first ancient musicians who used wood, rocks, animal skins—and their own bodies—to re-create the sounds of the natural world in which they lived. With their hands, their feet, and their very breath they ignited the passions of listeners and moved them to their feet. The dancing, in turn, had a mesmerizing and hypnotic effect that allowed people to transcend their worldly concerns. Through music they could achieve a level of shared experience that could not be found in other forms of communication. For this reason, music has always been part of religious endeavors, from ancient Egyptian spiritual ceremonies to modern Christian masses. And it has inspired dance movements from kings and queens spinning the minuet to punk rockers slamming together in a mosh pit.

By examining musical genres ranging from Western classical music to rock and roll, readers will find a new understanding of old music and develop an appreciation for new sounds. Books in Lucent's Music Library focus on the music, the musicians, the instruments, and on music's place in cultural history. The songs and artists examined may be easily found in the CD and sheet music collections of local libraries so that readers may study and enjoy the music covered in the books. Informative sidebars, annotated bibliographies, and complete indexes highlight the text in each volume and provide young readers with many opportunities for further discussion and research.

When All Music Was Classical

The term *classical* defines a style of Western music that began in Europe in the 1400s. The expression was originally used to describe the Viennese classical school, a group of eighteenth-century composers that includes Joseph Haydn, Wolfgang Amadeus Mozart, and Ludwig van Beethoven. In modern times, classical sounds also encompass thirteenth-century Gregorian chants, fifteenth-century Renaissance madrigals, twentieth-century classical-jazz suites by Igor Stravinsky, and the avant-garde electric sound pieces of composer Karlheinz Stockhausen.

Elements of Classical Music

Classical music is composed of several elements that help define its character. Because music takes place in time, rhythm is the foundation for every song. Like the beating of the heart, composers determine the feel of music by alternating the pulse, or rhythm, between fast, slow, and medium. Italian terms used in musical notation denote more than a dozen different tempos, or meters, for a piece, including *prestissimo*—very fast indeed; *allegro*—fast and cheerful; *moderato*—moderate tempo; *lento*—slow; and *grave*—very slow.

A treble clef made out of flowers decorates a memorial to Wolfgang Amadeus Mozart in Vienna, Austria. The term classical initially referred to eighteenth-century musicians of the Viennese school such as Mozart.

Within the changing meter of the rhythm, successions of expressive musical notes, or melodies, are intertwined. As British musicologists Stanley Sadie and Alison Latham note, "[Melody] is the heart of music; no aspect of musical skill is as much prized as the ability to compose melodies that are shapely, expressive and memorable."[1]

Timbre, or tone color, describes the characteristics that give each instrument its unique sound. Various timbres include the high-frequency treble of a blaring trumpet and the crashing clang of a cymbal. These tone colors affect the ear much differently than the low breathy tone of an oboe or light lilt of a string section. As classical music authorities Robert Sherman and Philip Seldon explain, "Sometimes the woodwinds predominate, sometimes the strings do; it's the composer's job to mix and match those separate tones until they produce the desired [orchestral color]."[2] Timbre, melody, and rhythm are all enhanced by *harmony*—the sound of two or more complementary notes played at the same time. Harmony makes melodies sound rich and full, accentuates changing rhythms, and gives each piece of music a unique character. When two or more harmonic melodies are played together it is known as *polyphony* (Greek for "many sounds"). This is opposed to *monophony*, music with a single dominant melody. Polyphony is also called *counterpoint*, which means point-against-point or note-against-note. (Another term for polyphony or counterpoint music is contrapuntal.) While these terms may seem confusing, counterpoint is demonstrated in its most basic form when a group of people sings "Row, Row, Row Your Boat." The song is performed in a round, that is, one person begins singing the first line after another person has just finished singing that line.

Music and Emotion

While terms like counterpoint, timbre, rhythm, and harmony define various aspects of music, they are so much more than technical concepts. When expertly combined by composers, these musical elements can generate tears, laughter, anger, serenity, excitement, and even terror in listeners.

In order to express strong emotions, classical composers have long based their work on classic fables, myths, and paintings. These literary and artistic works often feature idealistic heroes, supernatural experiences, and colossal battles between good and evil. For example, the musical piece "The Erl King" by Franz Schubert is based on a poem by Johann Wolfgang von Goethe. The poem takes place in a forest where a young boy's soul is stolen from him by an evil spirit.

Such stories have universal appeal, and over the centuries classical became everyone's music. The works of Mozart and Johannes Brahms may be heard everywhere from the speakers at a shopping mall to formal concerts in China. Classical albums featuring some of the finest classical works are available online and sold at stores for incredibly low prices. Internet and broadcast radio stations play commercial-free classical music twenty-four hours a day.

While musical tastes have changed over the decades, classical music has transcended fashion and found a permanent place in modern culture. With little effort, people may familiarize themselves with the evocative melodies of the masters and touch the universal human emotion that binds the past to the present—and individuals to one another.

CHAPTER 1

Medieval and Renaissance Roots

The origins of modern classical music evolved during the fifth century B.C. in ancient Greece. This era, known as the Greek classical period, saw a flowering of the arts, as philosophers, poets, and playwrights created works that are still revered today. Music often accompanied dance and dramatic plays as well as government and religious functions. Musicians at these celebrations played Greek versions of modern instruments such as a harp-like lyre, called the kithara, and the double-reed aulos, the forerunner of the oboe. It is believed that the music played at this time did not employ harmony and was generally improvised, or made up on the spot, by the musicians.

Greek civilization faded, and the powerful Roman Empire took its place in the first two centuries A.D. Roman emperors supported large orchestras and choruses, which featured extremely skilled musicians, or virtuosos. The Romans intertwined their songs with poems, verses, and words, while improvising musical lines.

Roman songs were considered more than just idle entertainment. Music was believed to be a powerful religious force, a phenomenon of nature produced by the gods. Music was used to sing the praises of deities, offer prayer, and cast supernatural spells. As British music critic William Mann writes, "Music, in early times, was a form of magic, inducing trance-like concentration in the listener. It soon became apparent that music had greater powers, and could be used as active propaganda to inspire a whole tribe, perhaps to bravery and war."[3]

The Influence of the Early Church

In A.D 325 the Roman Emperor Constantine made Christianity the official religion of Rome. In the centuries that followed, the course of music was directed and shaped by officials within the Christian church, and religious officials preached against the evils of secular, or non-religious, music. U.S. musicologist Donald J. Grout explains:

> Certain features of ancient musical life were definitely rejected—for example, the idea of [playing] music purely for enjoyment as an art. Above all, the forms and types of music connected with the great public spectacles such as festivals, competitions . . . [and] dramatic performances . . . were regarded by many as unsuitable for the Church.[4]

Leaders in the church believed that music should be limited mainly to the singing of prayers and psalms, or hymns. The church adapted ancient Jewish musical practices; particularly, the manner in which psalms were sung, a technique known as *responsorial psalmody*. During this type of holy song, a lead vocalist sang the first line of a psalm alone, and the congregation responded by singing the second line in unison.

As the influence of the Christian church spread through the Mediterranean regions of the Middle East, Africa, and Europe, the church incorporated the musical styles of the people who lived in those areas. In that manner, regional folk songs were melded with early hymns.

The Influence of Pope Gregory

In A.D. 600 Pope Gregory the Great decided to purge secular influences from psalms and hymns. The pope designated specific music for various church services throughout the seasons while eliminating music he considered profane or

A nineteenth-
century painting
depicts sixth-century
Pope Gregory I
teaching chants to
a group of students.
Pope Gregory
revolutionized
sacred music and
also developed
musical notation
to teach complex
melodies.

irreligious. The most important feature of Gregory's work was to make Mass the center of Christian religious services. As a ritual enactment of the Last Supper, masses were held on holidays such as Easter, Christmas, saints' birthdays, funerals (requiem masses), and other events. During these occasions the text of the Mass was chanted in Latin and some sections were sung.

In this era, before the advent of musical notation, Gregory needed a way to simplify the teaching of complex melodies to church choirs. The pope devised a method whereby he gave each note a letter of the alphabet. Gregory assigned various eight-note scales, or modes, names from ancient Greece. The modes included Dorian, Lydian, and Mixolydian. Together the modes were used in the singing of Gregorian chants, also known as *plainsong*, explained by music historian Dhun H. Sethna in *Classical Music for Everybody*:

[The] music of the entire Mass consisted of a single, re-petitively chanted line, trance-like and deeply mystical, [without] any instrumental accompaniment. . . . Only the unadorned human voice with a single-minded fo-cus of attention [was seen as] worthy enough to be-come a medium between heaven and earth.[5]

Each community had its own versions of Gregorian chants, and more than three thousand such melodies sur-vive today. Every plainsong originally had its own specific purpose during various church ceremonies, and many of these songs formed a basis for Christian religious music throughout the Middle Ages.

The influence of plainsong spread across Europe after Gregory established the Schola Cantorum, the first singing school in Rome where singers could learn the Gregorian chants. In the decades that followed, branches of the Schola Cantorum were opened in cities across Europe. As Grout explains, the schools helped preserve Gregorian music for hundreds of years:

The Gregorian chants . . . were the source and inspira-tion of a large portion of all Western music up to the sixteenth century. They constitute one of the most an-cient bodies of song still in use anywhere, and include some of the noblest artistic works ever created in pure melody.[6]

The Rise of Harmony

Gregorian chants consist only of melodies unaccompanied by harmony notes. Around the tenth century, church com-posers began adding harmony to the music. The new style was called *organum* because voices were accompanied by the organ, which was developed around the ninth century and widely used in churches throughout Europe.

Organum consists of three-part harmony. One person sings the main melody, and the second sings the same notes but an octave (eight notes) above or below the first. Meanwhile, a third person sings in the middle range, above or below the main melody. In later centuries the simple style of organum was embellished so that the different voices sang shorter or longer notes, resulting in a richly varied melody.

The Invention of Do-Re-Mi

As organum grew in popularity, a new method for teaching complex harmony to church choirs became necessary. Around A.D. 1030, this led to the invention of the familiar "do-re-mi" singing method by a choirmaster monk named Guido of Arezzo.

Guido developed names for six notes (C-D-E-F-G-A) based on a popular Latin hymn called "Ut Queant Laxis." He cleverly used the first two letters of the first words in each line to name the corresponding notes, ut-re-mi-fa-sol-la. (The verses of the song were *UT queant laxis, REsonare fibris, MIra gestorum, FAmuli tuorum, SOLve polluti, LAbii reatum*). The notes are taught the same way today, but ut has been replaced by do, and ti has been added after la.

In addition to the do-re-mi system, the monk developed another teaching aid known as the Guidonian Hand, so choirboys could learn to sight sing. Guido assigned one of twenty notes to the knuckles and joints of his hand and the tips of his fingers. Students could sing the notes as the monk pointed to the various parts of his left hand with his right index finger. This method of teaching proved to be so helpful that over the centuries a drawing of the Guidonian Hand was included in nearly every musical textbook.

Some have even speculated that each of the five lines of the modern musical staff, upon which musical notation is written, may represent Guido's fingers. Grout writes that the staff played an important role in the evolution of music: "The invention of the staff made it possible to notate precisely the . . . pitch of the notes of a melody, and freed music from its . . . exclusive dependence on oral transmission. It was an event as crucial for the history of Western music as the invention of writing was for the history of language."[7]

The Guidonian Hand, developed by Guido of Arezzo in the eleventh century, was used for centuries to teach music.

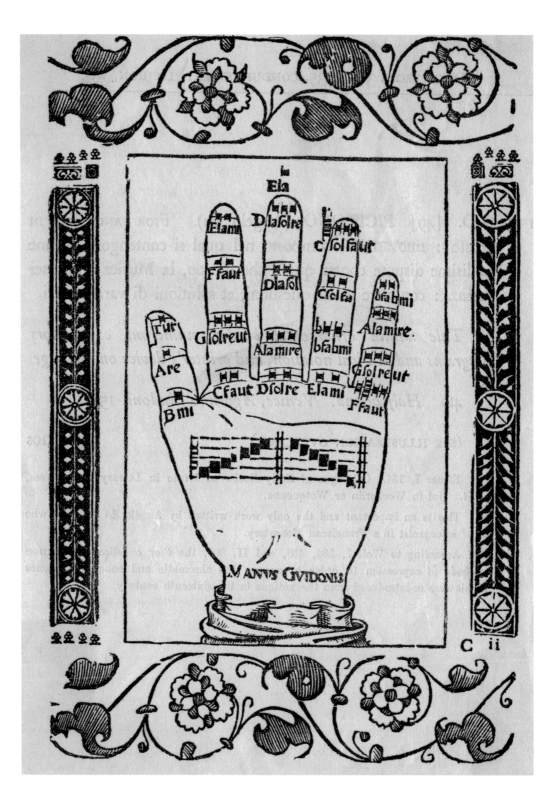

The Polyphonic Perspective

With the development of musical notation, original works of music could be made permanent and available to any player who could read the notes. The universal language of a musical score also allowed a piece to be taught to others no matter where they lived. As Grout writes, "The score . . . was a set of directions which could be executed whether or not the composer was present. Thus composition and performance became separate acts instead of being combined in one person as before."[8]

The art of composition also allowed music to take on a new characteristic referred to as *polyphony*. Polyphonic music consists of two or more different melodies that are combined to give songs a richness, strength, and power previously unheard in Western music. Two of the first composers of polyphonic music are Léonin, who lived in the 1170s, and Pérotin, who lived in the first part of the 1200s. Both men were choirmasters at the Notre Dame Cathedral in Paris. Their style of music, along with compositions by dozens of unknown composers, is referred to as the Notre Dame School.

Léonin's work is known throughout the world today because he wrote the *Magnus Liber Organi*, or the "Great Book of Organum," which is still in print. Léonin wrote mainly for two voices, but his book was later revised by Pérotin, who added three or even four voices to the works. The polyphonic songs of the Notre Dame School, according to Mann, are "soaring, magnificent and [resounding]—and . . . laid the foundation of a polyphonic style whose flowering was to last some 400 years."[9]

Motet

Organum has two distinct parts, and a new type of music known as *motet* evolved from one of these parts. The fixed melody of organum, called *fixity*, follows an unchanging part. The other part is called freedom, or *descant*, and describes the harmonious singing that weaves between the fixed melody. When Pérotin composed his polyphonic organums, he would oftentimes write dozens of freedom sections that a choir could sing over a single fixity section. Each freedom part varied in tempo, key, and musical color and could be used for specific rituals, depending on the mood desired. At first these freedom sections did not have words, but during the thirteenth century, sacred texts—and even secular poems—were added. Eventually freedom sections were recognized as unique songs separate from the organum from which they originated. Thousands of motets were written during the thirteenth century, and many are still sung today.

A Musical Rebirth

By the end of the 1300s, the concepts of melody, harmony, and rhythm developed in the church were spreading to the secular world. This occurred at a time when the Church was losing its dominant role in society due to an intellectual movement known as humanism. First popularized in Italy in the early 1400s, humanism is a belief system that emphasizes the personal worth of the individual—and the importance of human values—as opposed to religious dogma. With humanists calling church doctrine into question, composers, artists, and writers turned to classical Greek culture for spiritual inspiration. This led to a movement in music, art, and literature known as the Renaissance (French for "rebirth"), which lasted from approximately 1400 to 1600. With the new spirit of rebirth, secular music became the primary form of entertainment in Italy, as historian Will Durant explains:

> [Renaissance literature] conveys a picture of a people singing or playing music in their homes, at their work, on the street, in music academies, monasteries, nunneries, churches, in processions . . . and pageants, in religious or secular plays, in the lyric passages and interludes of dramas. . . . Rich men kept a variety of musical instruments in their homes, and arranged private [music programs]. Women organized clubs for the study and performance of music. Italy was mad about music. . . . Almost every Italian could

Musical Instruments of the Renaissance

Historian Will Durant describes the musical instruments of the Renaissance era:

Although nearly all music in this age was vocal, the accompanying instruments were as diverse as in a modern orchestra. There were string instruments like psalteries, harps, dulcimers, shawms [early oboes], lutes, and viols; wind instruments like flutes, oboes, bassoons, trumpets, trombones, cornets, and bagpipes; percussion instruments like drums, bells, clappers, cymbals, and castanets; keyboard instruments like organs, clavichords, harpsichords, spinets, virginals; there were many more. . . .

The favorite accompaniment for the single voice was the lute. . . . Usually its body was made of wood and ivory, and shaped like a pear; its belly was pierced with holes in the pattern of a rose; it had six—sometimes twelve—pairs of strings, which were plucked by the fingers . . . .

The viol differed from the lute in having its strings stretched over a bridge and played by a bow, but the principle was the same—the vibration of taut struck strings over a box perforated to deepen sound. . . . During the sixteenth century the viola da braccio evolved into the violin, and in the eighteenth the viol passed out of use.

Will Durant. *The Reformation: The Story of Civilization.* New York: Simon & Schuster, 2011, pp. 932–933.

A Renaissance painting by Michelangelo Merisi da Caravaggio shows a boy with a lute, the favorite accompaniment at the time for single voice.

sing, and nearly as many could sing in simple . . . harmony.[10]

Music was important to people of all social classes, and even the wealthy were not considered truly refined unless they knew how to read music and play an instrument. Kings, queens, and aristocrats were also major patrons of the musical arts. Large sums of money were spent to draw talented singers, musicians, and composers to royal courts. To further enhance musical culture, nobles supported a wide array of instrument makers who built finely crafted and artistic harpsichords, organs, lutes, and other instruments.

With so much attention focused on secular music, cathedrals dramatically improved their musical offerings to stay in step with the times. In major cities such as Venice, Milan, and Naples, churches competed fiercely with one another to attract the best singers, choir directors, organ players, and other musicians.

Guillaume Dufay

Ironically, while the Renaissance in Italy inspired a large number of musicians, painters, and sculptors across Europe, there were few Italian composers. Yet, the flowering of the arts in Italy, combined with the generous financial patronage of the nobility, attracted composers from the North, particularly northeastern France and Flanders (present-day Belgium). One of the most famous and widely imitated musical geniuses of the day was Guillaume Dufay. He was born around 1400 in the Burgundy region of central France, one of the most musically active areas of fifteenth-century Europe.

Dufay spent much of his life traveling Italy while absorbing Renaissance culture and contributing to the musical language of the era. He wrote dozens of secular songs in French concerning love, the beauty of nature, the pleasures of wine, and even the humorous aspects of fist-fighting.

Musically, Dufay was a master of harmony. He also relied on a technique called *dissonance* in which melodies are left unresolved, giving a musical phrase a feeling of drifting off into silence rather than ending with definite resolution.

A page from a sixteenth-century manuscript depicts Guillaume Dufay (left) and Gilles Binchois, two influential composers of the fifteenth century.

The Burgundian School

Dufay's music was widely published and performed throughout the cosmopolitan cities of Europe, and he composed for popes, dukes, and kings. Dufay also inspired his contemporaries, especially those in his home region of Burgundy. The Burgundian composers were noted for their sophisticated secular songs with lyrics called *chansons*, written for three-part harmony.

The center of the Burgundian school was the court of Duke Philip the Good, and later, that of his son Charles the Bold. Philip was a devoted patron of the musical arts and in 1506 employed as many as thirty-three court musicians—more than the powerful king of France. These players were singers, virtuoso instrumentalists, and composers. Philip the Good was devoted to secular music, and the musicians often played instruments such as bagpipes, trumpets, tambourines, primitive oboes, lutes, flutes, harps, and an early incarnation of the viol, known as the *veille*.

The Age of Guillaume Dufay

Belgian musicologist Charles Van den Borren describes the work of Guillaume Dufay, one of the foremost composers of the Renaissance period:

> Renowned for the greatness of his genius, Dufay's name was known to all. Sought after by the [rulers] of the earth, not only in the Church but also in the royal, princely, and baronial courts of the Burgundian [region] of France and of Italy, he moved about from youth to old age with the utmost freedom, riding over hill and dale from one court to another . . . [with] the Pope or the Duke of Savoy. . . .
>
> Thus it came about that he chronicled in song the affairs both great and small of Europe's social and religious life . . . . It is therefore not at all surprising that modern historians have described the first sixty years of the fifteenth century as "the age of Dufay." He was the dominating musical personality of the time, and he blazed the trail for his contemporaries and followers by the richness and variety of his [musical] inventions.

Quoted in Dom Anselm Hughes and Gerald Abraham (eds). *Ars Nova and the Renaissance 1300–1540.* Oxford, England: Oxford University Press, 1986, pp. 214–215.

Like most other rulers of the day, the duke was politically ruthless but, unlike many noblemen, a playful man in his own court. This was seen at the Feast of the Pheasant banquet on February 17, 1454, when Philip had his court musicians play while seated in a huge pie dish. This event might have been the inspiration for the English nursery rhyme "Sing a Song of Sixpence" with its verse "four and twenty blackbirds/baked in a pie./When the pie was opened/the birds began to sing."

Chansons of the Troubadours

The first ballads with secular lyrics were referred to by the word *chansons,* French for "song." Chansons were popular among educated aristocrats because the lyrics recalled the patriotic deeds and heroic actions of revered royals. Epic *chansons de geste,* or "songs of action," contained four thousand to fifteen thousand verses and were prevalent from about A.D. 800 to 1100. Chansons de geste were essentially musical history lessons. For example, the four thousand lines of the "Song of Roland" detail the eighth-century invasion of Spain by French King Charlemagne.

Chansons were hand copied on small manuscripts that could be carried by wandering minstrels, known as troubadours, in England. In other regions the singers were called gleemen, scops, jongleurs, or goliards. In Germany, troubadours were called minnesingers, or "singers about love." They were so-named because, in addition to writing and singing chansons de geste, the minstrels performed short, joyous love songs that celebrated courtly love. The lyrics often idolized women as beautiful and unattainable, which led to great heartache for the song's central character. The troubadours entertained rich and poor alike, singing solo or accompanying themselves with lutes, harps, and violin-like instruments known as the *lira da braccio.*

Although he never played in a pie dish, one of the foremost composers of the Burgundian School was Gilles Binchois, a singer and composer from Mons, Belgium. Binchois wrote more than fifty chansons for solo voice and two instruments. Many of these were quite advanced for their time, with the vocalist singing the melody line, the lowest instrument playing a droning sort of note, and the middle instrument completing the three-part harmonic chord.

The Netherlands School

Binchois was so revered that after his death in 1460, his deeds were commemorated in songs written by Dufay and the composer Johannes Ockeghem. Born in present-day Netherlands around 1425, Ockeghem was member of a generation of composers known as the Netherlands School. They worked between 1450 and 1550 during the era of flowering creativity referred to as the High Renaissance.

The music of the Netherlands School was inspired by the works of Dufay and Binchois. It was expanded upon by Ockeghem, who was known as the Prince of Music for his technical mastery of musical forms such as motet, religious masses, and chansons. Ockeghem utilized intricate four-part harmony, dramatic vocal bass parts, and complex counterpoint in demanding compositions that could only be played by the most skilled musicians.

When Ockeghem died in 1497, his life was celebrated in a musical lament written by one of his students, Josquin des Prez, another revered composer of the Netherlands School. Des Prez was French, but he worked for some of Italy's most powerful men in Milan, Rome, and Florence. The time spent in Italy colored his technically proficient Netherlands School music, giving it a more lighthearted sound that later came to be associated with all Renaissance music. The Italian influence in des Prez's sound is described by music authority Alec Harman:

> It was as if the southern sun had warmed and stirred the closed bud of his genius, causing it to unfurl until the full flower was revealed. . . . This emotional [music], expressed through sensuous harmony and

melodic lines . . . of great beauty . . . together with a profound technical skill . . . make him . . . one of the greatest composers of all time.[11]

Des Prez was among many composers who were renowned for their work in the sixteenth century, including Heinrich Isaac, Clément Janequin, and Orlande de Lassus. In Italy, Giovanni Pierluigi da Palestrina wrote such exquisite masses for unaccompanied voices that he too was known as the "Prince of Music."

Madrigals

The Burgundian and Netherlands School composers mainly wrote their complex music for kings, queens, aristocrats, and popes. The most common type of music enjoyed by average citizens in public squares and private homes was a vocal style known as *madrigal*.

Madrigals are songs written for three or more vocalists who sing *a cappella*, or without musical accompaniment. Like other novel artistic achievements that developed during the Renaissance, madrigals were actually based on an old style. In the fourteenth century, the Italian poet Petrarch wrote verses that were meant to be sung to music. These songs, originally called *frottole*, are stilted and repetitious. French composers in Italy, along with those in Germany and England believed the *frottole* did not do musical justice to Petrarch's sonnets. This inspired them to create the madrigal which, according to Mann, is "a more flexible, expressive and emotional sort of music."[12]

During the 1550s, thousands of madrigals were written in Italy alone. They were performed in private settings and at public events by groups of three to seven unaccompanied vocalists. The lyrics of the madrigals were meant to appeal to a wide audience, featuring an emotional mixture of love, sex, and death. The rhythms of the music were strongly

---

A page from a sixteenth-century manuscript shows Johannes Ockeghem in his chapel. Ockeghem's complex compositions required highly skilled musicians.

emphasized by dramatic words such as "anger" and "die" in what is known as "word painting."

The madrigal style was taken to England by Italian composer Alfonso Ferrabosco the elder. Ferrabosco was a member of Queen Elizabeth I's court, and his songs set off a madrigal fad that lasted from about 1588 to 1627. English madrigals were lighter and less sophisticated than those composed on the mainland of the European continent.

English Fa-La-La

The prominent English composer William Byrd was among the most popular madrigal writers. Byrd preferred a joyous version of the madrigal, known as the *ballett*, which featured repetitive verses and a "fa-la-la" refrain. For example, Byrd's composition "May" is sung, "Now is the month of may-ing / When merry lads are playing / fa-la la la la la la la, fa-la la la la la la."[13]

Byrd's madrigals, along with so many others, are part of the Renaissance tradition that has survived the centuries. While sounding quaint to modern ears, the music, like the era in which it was played, was revolutionary. On a cultural and social level, the music grew and changed with the times, from serious liturgical masses to rollicking bawdy chansons and madrigals.

While the dual paths of secular and religious music were often separated during the Renaissance, the distinct styles would intersect periodically during the centuries that followed. This duality of popular songs and spiritual music would continue to inspire composers and build the foundations for classical music well into the modern age.

CHAPTER 2

The Baroque Era

At the end of the Renaissance era, European music had developed to include styles such as chanson, madrigal, and the intricate polyphonic music written by composers of the Netherlands School. In this period of musical development, there was also a great leap forward in the quality and quantity of musical instruments. During the late Renaissance, improved versions of instruments such as the flute, trumpet, trombone, violin, cello, and organ emerged. The best instruments were made by highly skilled Renaissance craftsmen. Because they were built to more exacting standards, the instruments stayed in tune better than those of earlier eras and produced richer timbres. With more high-quality instruments available, composers were able to move beyond the vocal-based songs of sixteenth century and write music for larger orchestras. This new style of music was called *baroque.*

With a wide range of tone colors available in their musical palettes, baroque composers created complex, ornamental works of musical art. The philosophical canvas on which these works were created originated in classical Greece where philosophers viewed music as a powerful tool of communication capable of inspiring listeners to emotional highs and lows.

The "Bizarre" Style of Baroque

The baroque era lasted from approximately 1600 to 1750. While baroque remains some of the most studied, played, and celebrated classical music, the term itself is an odd choice to describe the sound. In English, the word *baroque* is derived from the Italian *barocco*, meaning "bizarre." This may be traced back to the Portuguese term *barroco*, a word used for an irregularly shaped or misshapen pearl.

The word was originally applied to the musical style in the 1730s by French poet Jean-Baptiste Rousseau, who scornfully mocked one composer as having written a piece that used "baroque chords of which so many idiots are enamored."[14] Rousseau criticized Italian composers once again in the 1750s, saying that they wrote music that was "bizarre and baroque." The term was finally immortalized in the 1760s when Rousseau wrote a widely read dictionary of music in which he defined baroque as music "in which harmony is confused, charged with modulations and dissonances, in which the melody is harsh and little natural, intonation difficult and the movement constrained."[15] Critics of baroque music such as Rousseau believed it was overdone, clumsy, and strange.

Despite this dubious beginning, the original meaning of the term was eventually forgotten. By the nineteenth century, baroque was a label given to elaborate and highly decorative art, architecture, and music created after the Renaissance and before the death of composer Johann Sebastian Bach in 1750.

Expressing Emotion

The early baroque period was influenced by Italian concepts of emotional expression. Baroque composers heightened passion and drama with sudden changes in tempo. Songs played very fast brought joy; those with short pauses or odd rhythms created tension. Slow music conveyed sadness.

In the most complex pieces, different tempos were played at the same time. This music, with deliberately contrasting elements, was called concerto. In a concerto, one

The Sonata

The musical form of the sonata became popular during the baroque era. British music critic William Mann explains sonatas:

A sonata is essentially music "sounded"—[that is] played, rather than sung (cantata). How long does a sonata last? Domenico Scarlatti's hundreds of harpsichord sonatas are in one short movement lasting about three minutes . . . . Beethoven's *Hammerklavier* sonata for piano lasts over half an hour, some modern examples even longer. In Italy the sonata settled, during the seventeenth century, into a free-formed piece of several contrasted sections, usually for violin, or two violins, and continuo [a keyboard accompaniment]. A distinction was at first made between the *sonata da chiesa* (for performance in church) and the *sonata da camera* (to be played at court, perhaps in a cultured home) . . . . By the early 1700s the distinction began to fade and the domestic sonata had acquired the same characteristics as the church variety.

It was [composer Arcangelo] Corelli . . . working in Rome, who, from 1681 standardized the number and length of the movements, which he kept separate. The keyboard solo sonata originated in Germany . . . as an instrumental work in several movements. The sonata travelled from Italy into Germany and other European countries.

William Mann. *James Galway's Music in Time.* New York: Henry N. Abrams, 1982, p. 90.

section of the orchestra, such as the woodwinds, might play a slow somber movement. Another section, such as the strings, simultaneously plays a rapid cascade of notes. This technique can create manic feelings or eerie frightful moods.

Contrasts could also be enhanced by manipulating volume. A very loud passage might excite the audience and convey enthusiasm or anger, depending on the piece. A section might end abruptly only to be followed by an extremely quiet movement that pushed listeners to the edges of their seats as they strained to hear the music.

Attending the First Opera

Dafne was the first opera ever produced, debuting in Florence, Italy, in 1597. Music scholar and author David Ewen describes the scene at the premiere:

The auditorium was a brilliantly lit salon in [composer] Jacopo Corsi's palace. The splendor of this setting was hardly more awesome than the social position of the audience, all of whom were of the nobility, come by invitation. Backstage, the composer was putting on his costume, for in his opera he was assuming the role of Apollo.

The curtains parted. An old Greek legend, its theme the last word in ingenuousness, came to life. Dafne (or Daphne) is pursued by the god Apollo. To protect Dafne, her mother transforms the girl into a laurel tree, which then becomes sacred to Apollo. That's the whole story. Surely the production would have been unremarkable, but for one important fact. The three characters—Dafne, Apollo, and Dafne's mother—sang rather than spoke their lines . . . . Further interest was contributed by the fact

Opera Brings Fables to Life

The elements used during the baroque period were also prominent in opera, a new musical form that began to develop at the end of the 1500s. The ancient Greek belief in music as emotional communication was best expressed when a single vocalist sang before an orchestra. With their voices and body movements, singers could express dramatic themes such as love, grief, anger, and regret in ways instrumental pieces could not.

A single voice with a simplified instrumental accompaniment is called *monody*. During the early 1600s monody was popular among composers who wrote hundreds of pieces about the expectations and disappointments of love. These songs allowed vocalists to capture the hearts of their audiences with sentimental singing.

The development of monody led a group of composers to lay the groundwork for modern opera in Florence, Italy. In the late sixteenth century, about a dozen poets, writers, that the voices and the dances were accompanied by instruments: a harpsichord (the precursor of the piano) or organ, lutes, old-time flutes, and a bass viol (forerunner of the cello). This new art form for the stage made a profound impression on its first audience.

David Ewen. *Opera.* New York: Franklin Watts, 1972, p. 9.

The Greek mythological story of Daphne and Apollo was the basis for the first opera ever produced. Peter Paul Rubens painted his version of the story in 1636.

musicians, and composers, known as *camerata*, or "men who meet in a chamber," gathered at the palace of a local count. The goal of the camerata was to revive ancient Greek stage dramas in which tragedies were acted out in song and dance. Music scholar and author David Ewen describes the work of the camerata:

The members of the *camerata* . . . felt strongly that if sixteenth-century Florentine poets were to write plays in the true spirit of Greek dramas, the texts must be supplied with music. This addition posed [a large] problem. After all, the prevailing music style of the time was still polyphony, and polyphony was . . . [not effective in] presenting [an understandable song]. You cannot have several people sing at the same time throughout a work and have the audience comprehend the words. And so, the *camerata* devised a new music style of one solo voice singing in a form of exaggerated speech. . . . This singing-speaking style, called *stile rappresentativo* [theater style], was probably close to what we hear in opera today.[16]

Working with the idea of speaking through music, composer Jacopo Peri created the first opera in 1597 from a story called *Dafne,* which was based on ancient Greek mythology. Because the term *opera* had not yet been coined, *Dafne* was referred to as a "fable in music" or "drama through music."[17] (The term opera came into common use in the early 1600s. It is taken from the Latin word for "work" as in "work of art.")

The new combination of drama and music was an instant success, and within a few years Peri was hired by King Henry IV of France to write an opera for the royal wedding. This production, called *Euridice,* is also based on Greek mythology and features the character Orpheus.

While Peri is credited with writing the first musical dramas, his work has little resemblance to operas of later years. As Ewen says, Peri's work "is primitive by any standards. The text is naïvely conceived. . . . Most of the singing is . . . little more than stylized speech."[18]

The Triumph of Monteverdi

Within a few years, the nobility grew tired of the slow wooden droning of Peri's work. Opera might have died a short time after its birth, were it not for the genius of Claudio Monteverdi, born in 1567 in Cremona, Italy. Monteverdi was a virtuoso violin player and wrote his first madrigals at the age of seventeen. By the time he was in his early twenties, he was playing viol and violin in the palace orchestra of the Duke of Mantua in northern Italy.

Working with the court poet in Mantua, Monteverdi's first opera, *La Favola d'Orfeo* (*The Fable of Orpheus*), premiered in February 1607. Ewen praises the opera: "It was a triumph. The audience could not fail to be stirred by the drama, made so compelling through Monteverdi's music. . . . Through great tonal leaps in the vocal line (sometimes to express grief, sometimes excitement), Monteverdi intensifies the emotions."[19]

In addition to the unique vocal arrangements, Monteverdi's musical score calls for a large, forty-one-piece orchestra. This was the first time a modern-style orchestra had been used. According to Stanley Sadie and Alison Latham, Monteverdi required: "Two harpsichords, two small wooden organs and a reed organ, a harp, two large lutes, three bass viols, ten violins and two small violins, two instruments like small double basses, four each of trumpets and trombones, two cornetts and two recorders."[20] The instruments were used in distinctive ways to express emotion. Strings, flutes, and the harpsichord create a musical backdrop for pastoral fields filled with nymphs. Trumpets and other brass instruments gave voice to creatures of the underworld.

Orfeo quickly made Monteverdi one of the most respected composers of the day. Professional musicians

Composer Claudio Monteverdi, seen in a portrait from around 1600, popularized opera in his native Italy.

throughout Italy learned to perform his works. As a result, opera became more accessible to average citizens and, for the first time, large numbers of public theaters were built. For example, in Venice there were no opera houses in 1630 but more than a dozen by 1637.

The popularity of opera drove developments in baroque music throughout Europe. During the first three-quarters of the seventeenth century, composers in Germany, England, and France took to writing Italian-style operas for the nobles who employed them, as music professor George J. Buelow explains:

> [By] the end of the century [opera] had become the most important and popular type of musical entertainment in the German courts, in the city of Hamburg, at the court of [French king] Louis XIV and, in the early eighteenth century, in London. Viewed from one perspective the history of the late Baroque [music] unfolds through the impact of operatic styles and forms on all music, sacred and secular.[21]

The Rise of Organ Music

Although secular opera was gaining in popularity, a style of organ-based, religious music was flourishing in Germany and other northern European locales. Pipe organs are large, expensive, and complicated instruments. Nevertheless, almost every middle-sized or large church owned an organ by the late 1600s. These churches employed organists who were expected to write original compositions for services.

Dieterich Buxtehude, born in Denmark in 1637, was one of the most versatile organists of the baroque era. Buxtehude spent most of his life in Lübeck in northern Germany where he gave public concerts at Saint Mary's Church. The recitals attracted musicians from towns and villages throughout Germany. Buxtehude's presentations also attracted promising musicians. In 1705, Bach, a twenty-five-year-old organist, attended one of Buxtehude's concerts and studied with him for four months.

Buxtehude was famous for his *oratorios*, grand works for voice, chorus, and orchestra often based on biblical texts. Perhaps the works that most impressed Bach were Buxtehude's *toccatas*—brilliant pieces of rapid music designed to let the organist show off his technique and touch on the keyboard.

The Musical Bachs

Buxtehude had a profound influence on Johann Sebastian Bach, who is revered as the master of baroque music. Ironically, throughout his lifetime, Bach remained a regional composer and was little known outside of Germany. Even in his native land, Bach was mainly recognized not as a composer but as an organ virtuoso—and an organ designer and repairman.

When Bach was born in the central German state of Thuringia on March 21, 1685, his family already had produced several generations of well-known skilled musicians. In fact, the name Bach was used interchangeably with the word musician in the region because there were thirty Bachs working as organists in Germany in the 1600s.

Coming from such a large musical family, Bach learned to play violin as soon as he could hold the instrument. By the time he was a teenager, he could sing and play organ, harpsichord, and other keyboard instruments. (The piano was not invented until around 1710, and such an instrument probably did not reach Germany until Bach was around twenty-five years old.)

Despite his talents, Bach did not have an easy experience as a musician. As Robert Sherman and Philip Seldon write, "He had to kiss up to his bosses to hold a job, he got in constant trouble with the authorities [for his musical experimentation], and when he wasn't turning out cantatas (more than 400 of them), he was producing children—at least 20 of them (although 13 of them died in infancy)."[22]

Bach's first brush with critics of his music came after he spent four months studying with Buxtehude. Bach's experience gave him exciting new melodic ideas that he played for the surprised and bewildered congregation upon returning to work as the church organist in Arnstadt. He was called before the church council and reprimanded, first for his

The Music of Bach

Classical music authorities Robert Sherman and Philip Seldon describe some of the greatest works composed by Johann Sebastian Bach:

> Almost everything Bach wrote is worthy of high attention, so where do we begin? Perhaps with the *Brandenburg Concertos*, those six magical works that were never performed during Bach's lifetime, but which are now an indelible part of . . . concert life. Each one has its own special instrumental timbre: no. 2, for instance, has solo parts for flute, violin, oboe, and high trumpets; no. 3 is for strings alone; no. 5 features the harpsichord, and so forth.
>
> Then try the two Violin Concertos and the Concerto for Two Violins; take an international sampling of keyboard pieces with the *French and English Suites* and the *Italian Concerto*. Listen to the six great sonatas and partitas for violin alone . . . .
>
> On the vocal scene, take a few hours off and be inspired by the B Minor Mass; or for lighter listening, sip a bit of the *Coffee Cantata*. Bach was justly renowned for his mastery of counterpoint, but if you seek gorgeous melody, pure and simple, try "Sheep May Safely Graze" or "Jesu, Joy of Man's Desiring," the latter providing a spiritual uplift into the bargain.

Robert Sherman and Philip Seldon. *The Complete Idiot's Guide to Classical Music.* New York: Alpha, 1997, p. 158.

four-month absence, and also for his new style of playing, which went against the strict traditional styles practiced in church. The words of the council were recorded in Charles Sanford Terry's *Johann Sebastian Bach*:

Complaints have been made . . . that you now accompany the hymns with surprising variations and irrelevant ornaments, which obliterate the melody and confuse the congregation. If you desire to introduce a theme against the melody, you must go on with it and not immediately fly off to another. And under no circumstances must you introduce a *tonus contrarius* [tone conflicting with the melody].[23]

"The Audacity of Genius"

Bach first gained notice for his music in 1708 when he composed "Gott Ist Mein König" ("God Is My King"). The piece is a *cantata*, or a vocal and instrumental work composed of choruses and solos. The cantata was composed to celebrate the inauguration of the Arnstadt town council. Sadly, "God Is My King" is the only one of Bach's four hundred cantatas that was ever published in his lifetime.

In June 1708, Bach moved to the small town of Weimar where the duke of Sachsen-Weimar offered him a position among his court chamber musicians. Following the trend of the baroque era, the court orchestra was large for its time. It consisted of twenty-two musicians: a compact string ensemble, a bassoon player, six trumpeters, and a timpani player. Bach mainly played violin, but he also filled in on harpsichord and wrote and arranged music. As was the custom in courts at that time, the musicians also spent time doing various household duties, and Bach, like the other musicians, was given a servant's uniform to wear.

At Weimar, Bach was free to compose, and during this time he wrote many of his great organ works. When these pieces were published, Bach gained a well-deserved reputation throughout Germany, and students flocked to his home to take lessons from the master.

Bach remained in the court orchestra for almost nine years. In 1717, the duke's orchestra master, or Kapellmeister, died, and Bach, who was in line for the job was passed over, prompting him to quit. He was soon hired as Kapellmeister for the young music-loving Prince Leopold at the small court of Cöthen where he worked for five years.

In the idyllic atmosphere of Cöthen, Bach was completely devoted to music. He spent his days writing chamber music, violin concertos, sonatas, and keyboard music.

He composed six concertos dedicated to Prince Christian Ludwig, margrave of Brandenburg. The *Brandenburg Concertos* are some of Bach's most famous compositions, and according to humanitarian and musicologist Albert Schweitzer,

> [The *Brandenburg Concertos*] have not one but several groups of solo instruments that are played . . . against each other in the development of the movement. The wind instruments are used with the audacity of genius. In the first concerto Bach employs, besides the strings, a wind-*ensemble* consisting of two horns, three oboes and bassoon; in the second, flute, oboe, trumpet and violin are used as a kind of solo quartet against the body of the strings; in the third he aims at no contrast of *timbres*, but employs three string trios, all constituted in the same way; in the fourth concerto the concertino consists of one violin and two flutes; in the fifth it consists of clavier, flute and violin; in the sixth, Bach employs only the *timbre* effects to be had from the strings,—two violas, two [bowed stringed instruments called the viola de gamba], and cello.[24]

Bach's Passion

While Bach may have had the "audacity of genius," in an ironic twist of fate, the margrave did not have the resources to hire an orchestra to play the *Brandenburg Concertos*. Bach was never able to hear the works performed during his lifetime.

Even after composing the magnificent concertos that went on to become the most beloved works of the nineteenth and twentieth centuries, Bach could not gain respect from church elders. When he applied for a job as music director at St. Thomas Church in Leipzig, he was passed over for another baroque composer, Georg Philipp Telemann. It was only after Telemann turned down the job that Bach was hired.

In Leipzig, Bach was forced to take on a busy work schedule teaching singing classes, attending cantata rehearsals,

overseeing Sunday and weekday services in the churches, and providing choirs for services in a local hospital and prison. In spite of his workload, Bach provided a complete set of cantatas for every Sunday service for more than five years.

In 1727 Bach wrote *St. Matthew Passion*, based on the Bible, in which characters such as Jesus, Peter, Pilate, and Judas all sing solos. A narrator tells the story and traditional hymns are mixed in between arias (solo vocal pieces). Although the works were relatively well received, Bach brought controversy upon himself in some quarters for making church music sound too much like opera. It was not until the nineteenth century that the genius of these pieces was recognized.

Today Bach is considered so important that musical historians have chosen July 28, 1750, the date of his death at the age of sixty-six, to mark the end of the musical era known as baroque. Yet, the greatness of his work was not fully realized until 1829 when composer Felix Mendelssohn revived

Johann Sebastian Bach was painted with his sons in 1730. Bach came from a large musical family and musical virtuosity also extended to his children.

St. Matthew Passion. In the 1850s, Bach's surviving works were published and promoted by the Bach Gesellschaft, or Bach Society, founded by musicians and scholars in Germany. By the end of the nineteenth century, Bach was widely considered one of the most prolific musicians of the baroque era and one of the greatest composers of all time.

Handel's Hallelujah

While Bach stands as the giant among baroque composers, he was not the only genius of his time. George Frideric Handel, born in Saxony, Germany, in 1685, received more recognition for his organ pieces—and earned a far better living—than Bach.

Handel was a violinist who composed his first opera, *Almira,* at the age of twenty. He traveled to Italy in 1706 where he worked in Florence and Venice composing op-

An illustration depicts George Frideric Handel presenting his Water Music Suite *to the English king George I. The piece was written to be played from a barge in the Thames River.*

era, church, and theatre music. Handel moved to London in 1710 and composed the opera *Rinaldo,* which premiered the following year. *Rinaldo,* a story of love and redemption that takes place in the eleventh century, was the first Italian-language opera performed on the English stage. *Rinaldo* made Handel an opera icon in England. During the decades that followed, the composer created several other celebrated operas including *Julius Caesar, Partenope,* and *Serse.*

Handel relied on royal patronage and worked for Queen Anne and King George I of England. One of Handel's most famous pieces, *Water Music Suite,* was written in 1717 at the request of George I who wanted something to listen to as he socialized with his friends.

Handel liked to work quickly, and his most famous piece, *Messiah,* was composed in only twenty-four days. Written in 1741, *Messiah* is an oratorio with scriptural text taken from the Bible. The rousing "Hallelujah Chorus," which concludes Part II of *Messiah* is among the most famous pieces of baroque music in the world. This choir piece, with its celestial soaring vocals is frequently heard around Christmas. The song even inspired its composer. Handel said that when he wrote "Hallelujah Chorus," "I saw all heaven before me, and the great God himself."[25]

Vivaldi's Expressions

While Handel's operatic work was respected, his output was small when compared to Antonio Vivaldi, born in Venice in 1678. Although Vivaldi taught music in an all-girls orphanage his entire career, he found the time to compose forty operas. Drawing on the influence of Renaissance folk music, Vivaldi also wrote energetic and rhythmic concertos for mandolin, lute, and guitar, as well as the flute, oboe, and violin. He composed nearly forty concertos for the bassoon alone.

Vivaldi's most famous work, *The Four Seasons,* is four concertos that musically illustrate the seasons. The work is expressive and playful, as Sherman and Seldon write: "Listen carefully . . . and you'll find a marvelous example of descriptive music, with clever images of twittering birds, burbling

Antonio Vivaldi enjoyed a prolific career as a composer. Among his violin concertos, The Four Seasons *is his most famous.*

brooks, snoozing shepherds, chattering teeth, horses at the hunt, and pelting hailstorms."[26]

By the time the baroque era ended in 1750, composers such as Vivaldi, Handel, and Bach had transformed the genre of classical music. In the beginning of the era, most pieces were written for small vocal and instrumental ensembles. At the end of the baroque period, orchestral and choral pieces had become grandiose, dramatic, and ornate and were performed by dozens of musicians and singers. During the same period, musically sophisticated opera came to be embraced by rich and poor, old and young. From the simple monody of the post-Renaissance period to the glorious power of Handel's *Messiah*, baroque era composers left a long-lasting impression upon the history of music.

CHAPTER 3

The Classical Period

In 1812, music critic E.T.A. Hoffmann wrote, "Haydn, Mozart, and Beethoven have developed a new art, whose origins first appear in the middle of the eighteenth century."[27] The "new art" Hoffmann referred to is a genre now known as classical music, a style composed from about 1750 to 1820.

While historians divide musical eras into neat categories, the music itself followed no such tidy timeline. Musicians of the classical era were influenced by Johann Sebastian Bach and likely viewed their compositions as a natural evolution of his baroque style. According to Robert Sherman and Philip Seldon:

Beethoven played several pieces from Bach's *Well-Tempered Clavier* . . . Mozart made string transcriptions of Bach pieces and wrote to his father that he had finally found music with something to teach him. Perhaps [composer Hector] Berlioz summed it up best when he wrote to a friend that "Bach is Bach, just as God is God."[28]

Along with Bach's influence, classical music was advanced by a relatively new instrument, the pianoforte. As a precursor to the modern piano, the pianoforte was invented by Italian instrument maker Bartolomeo Cristofori in 1710. The instrument was first mass produced in Germany,

Classical music was advanced by Bartolomeo Cristofori's invention of the pianoforte. The oldest surviving pianoforte (pictured) is currently in the collection of the Metropolitan Museum of Art in New York City.

Austria, and England in the 1760s. The pianoforte could produce loud or soft notes depending on how hard the keys were struck. Joseph Haydn, Wolfgang Amadeus Mozart, and Ludwig van Beethoven were all masters of the pianoforte and utilized the expressive tones of the instrument in a variety of ways. The pianoforte could be used to play quiet solo pieces or loud chords with a full orchestra. In addition, with its four-octave range, the pianoforte was a composer's dream, ideal for writing numerous parts for a variety of orchestral instruments.

Enlightened Thinking

The advances in classical music occurred during an era known as the Enlightenment, a cultural movement that wielded a powerful influence on composers and other artists. The philosophers of the Enlightenment were deeply inspired by science while strongly rejecting the unbending religious dogma of the Church. Enlightenment thinkers supported artistic self-expression, free from censorship by church or state. They opposed religious intolerance and the repression of the people by the totalitarian kings and princes who ruled Europe. Enlightenment writers, musicians, and artists dreamed of a society where truth would triumph over ignorance, reason over superstition, and liberty and freedom would topple oppressive despotism.

The influence of the Enlightenment on classical music may be seen in the notable decline of religious compositions. This was accompanied by a sharp rise in the popularity of secular music written specifically for middle-class audiences rather than the nobility. Overall, the Enlightenment inspired classical composers to write music that was logical, intelligent, and balanced.

Elegant Symphonic Music

During the Enlightenment, there was an emphasis on learning and self-improvement. This created a trend in which countless average citizens picked up instruments and learned to play music at home. Classical composers were able to take advantage of this situation by writing music that was elegant and interesting—yet simple enough for amateurs to play. This allowed composers to earn respectable incomes publishing their pieces in lesson books. The trend was also seen in opera, where vocal songbooks were popular among people who wanted to sing songs at home that they had enjoyed in the theater. Using these books, refined young women learned to play the piano, harpsichord, while young men picked up the violin, oboe, or flute. Professional musicians augmented their incomes by giving lessons in peoples' homes.

The shift in music from the complex and mysterious to the simple and elegant was advanced by the form known as *style galant*, or *galant*. This style was characterized by free-flowing melodies that were not complicated by the rhythms of counterpoint. Galant songs featured light instrumentation that provided a backdrop to the main melody. According to

Stanley Sadie and Alison Latham, "The ideal medium for galant melody was the singing voice, in a cantata or an operatic song (preferably on an amorous text). . . . Another popular medium was the flute . . . which was specially esteemed for its capacity for elegant and tender shading."[29]

Concert Life

During the Enlightenment, music became more accessible to the average person, and the first public concerts were performed in Europe. British musicologists Stanley Sadie and Alison Latham describe this phenomenon:

It was in the eighteenth century that concert life began as we know it. In earlier times instrumental music was chiefly intended for performance at court or for groups of gentleman amateurs to play in their homes. Now a new phenomenon arose. Groups of people, often of both amateurs and professionals, got together to give concerts for their own pleasure . . . and for the pleasure of others who came to hear them. In larger cities, where more professionals were to be found, orchestral concerts were regularly given. London and Paris led, and others were quick to follow . . . . Concert life developed rapidly; traveling virtuosos went from city to city, organizing concerts . . . . The orchestra as an entity began to take firm shape. The concept of a public that came to concerts to listen was a novel one, demanding a novel approach to composition; it was more than ever necessary for a piece of music to have a logical and clearly perceptible shape, so that it would grasp and hold the listener's attention and interest.

Stanley Sadie and Alison Latham, eds. *The Cambridge Music Guide.* Cambridge, England: Cambridge University Press, 2000, p. 222.

Style galant was performed by a new type of orchestral configuration, the string quartet, composed of two violins, a cello, and a viola—a stringed instrument tuned an octave above the cello. Style galant was also played by much larger orchestras composed of keyboards, woodwind, brass, string, and (occasionally) percussion sections. These types of orchestras were labeled symphony, from the Greek term "sounding together."

Symphony not only defined the orchestra but a new type of musical arrangement invented by classical composers. The first symphonies are made up of three songs, or movements, of various lengths. (Most modern symphonies have four movements.) Early symphonies are standardized into two styles: The three movements written in the French style feature tempos played slow-quick-slow; Italian style is played quick-slow-quick.

The Mannheim Rocket

Early composers did not have organized orchestras to play their symphonies. They simply assembled whatever musicians were available when it was time to give a performance. This gave the music an amateurish sound, produced by musicians who had little practice playing together. This problem was solved in the mid-eighteenth century, when the foundation of the modern professional symphony orchestra was laid by violinist Johann Stamitz in the southern German city of Mannheim.

Stamitz was hired by the city's music-loving ruler Karl Theodor to act as concertmaster in the Mannheim court. Stamitz, from what is now the Czech Republic, composed as many as seventy symphonies despite the fact that he died at the age of forty.

Stamitz's symphonies became instantly popular throughout Europe and attracted hundreds of composers and musicians to Mannheim. This resulted in the foundation of the Mannheim School, which grew up around Stamitz's talents. Sherman and Seldon describe the sounds of Stamitz:

> [His] orchestra pioneered gradations of sound that had been unknown before—swellings of volume

(crescendo) and its opposite (diminuendo), a kind of drooping figure that became known as the "Mannheim Sigh" and a leaping group of notes nicknamed the "Mannheim Rocket." Local composers, members of the . . . Mannheim School, wrote pieces to take special advantage of these exciting orchestral possibilities, and by showing the world what creative imagination, effective leadership, and high performing discipline could accomplish, the Mannheimers gave the symphony orchestra a completely new significance in the musical world.[30]

Because they were supported by nobility with somewhat limited funds, the symphony orchestras of the Mannheim era were much smaller than modern configurations, which may have well over one hundred musicians. In the mid-1750s, the Mannheim orchestra had only forty-five members. (Average baroque orchestras featured around twenty-four players.)

Franz Joseph Haydn: "Father of the Symphony"

While Stamitz originated the modern symphony orchestra, Franz Joseph Haydn's huge contribution to the symphonic style earned him the name "Father of the Symphony."[31] Born in 1732 to an impoverished family in a small town in eastern Austria, Haydn spent almost thirty years in the position of Kapellmeister at a provincial court outside of Vienna. While working for Prince Nicholas "the Magnificent" Esterházy, who owned twenty-one castles, Haydn spent most of his life in the prince's luxurious two-hundred-room palace in the remote countryside of Eisenstadt.

From 1761 to 1790—the height of the classical era—Haydn conducted the twenty-five-member royal orchestra and a dozen singers while composing operas, chamber music, ceremonial pieces, and other works for the prince. In addition to writing an original composition per week, the Kapellmeister's job required him to coach the singers, fix broken instruments, and make sure the musicians, some of the finest in Europe, were properly groomed and arrived at work on time. Because the prince played the viola-like instrument known as the baryton, Haydn composed more than two hundred pieces for that stringed instrument.

Although his workload kept him busy, Haydn believed he was lucky to be able to write music continually without interruptions or restrictions. As the composer told his biographer before his death,

My Prince was content with all my works, I received approval, I could, as head of an orchestra, make experiments, observe what enhanced an effect, and what weakened it, thus improving, adding to, cutting away, and running risks. I was set apart from the world, there was nobody in my vicinity to confuse and annoy me in my course, and so I had to be original.[32]

"Forever New and Surprising"

Haydn was so prolific during this period that he wrote an astounding 106 symphonies, 68 string quartets, 60 piano sonatas, 25 operas, 4 oratorios, and countless songs, arias, cantatas, overtures, concertos, serenades, trios, and chamber works.

Some of the names Haydn gave his symphonies demonstrated his sly sense of humor. For example, No. 83 is nicknamed *The Hen* because the first movement features oboes and violins making "clucking" sounds. William Mann lists the titles for some other symphonies and how they earned their names:

[The] *Surprise*, no. 94 (a loud chord to awake sleepy listeners), the *Miracle*, no. 96 (a glass chandelier fell and broke in the concert-room, but hurt nobody because the audience, carried away by the power of the music, had crowded to the edge of the . . . [stage]) . . . ; The *Farewell* symphony, no. 45 in F sharp minor, was composed as a reminder to the Prince that his musicians were impatient to return home to Vienna: in the finale, the players stop playing one by one, snuff out the candles on their music-desks and leave the platform, until finally only two solo violins are left playing in

Haydn's Courtly Life

When Franz Joseph Haydn was hired to work for the German prince Nicholas "the Magnificent" Esterházy, he was given a contract with a set of royal instructions he was expected to follow to the letter. It stated that Haydn had to settle the quarrels among his musicians, look after the instruments, and rehearse the female singers. The original contract states even more conditions:

[Joseph Haydn] will be temperate, and will know that he must treat the musicians placed under him not overbearingly, but with mildness and leniency, modestly, quietly and honestly . . . appearing neatly in white stockings, white linen, powdered, and either with pigtail or hair-bag [a wig accessory]. . . .

[The] Capel-Meister shall be under permanent obligation to compose such pieces of music as his Serene Princely Highness may command, and neither to communicate such new compositions to anyone, nor to allow them to be copied, but to retain them wholly for the exclusive use of his Highness; nor shall he compose for any other person without the knowledge and gracious permission [of his Highness].

Quoted in H. C. Robbins Landon, ed. *Haydn, A Documentary Study*. New York: Rizzoli, 1981, p. 42.

This concert hall at the court of Prince Nicholas "the Magnificent" Esterházy is the venue where many of Joseph Haydn's symphonies and operas were first performed.

the extravagant key of F sharp major. The Prince is reported to have understood the message.[33]

While under the prince's patronage, Haydn had little idea of how famous and respected he was throughout Europe; by the 1770s, his published sheet music was selling at a rapid rate. When the prince died in 1790, Haydn traveled to London where he was hired by promoter Johann Peter Salomon to write a dozen new symphonies and conduct concerts. In England, the composer quickly became an instant celebrity. His concerts were so enthusiastically received that cheering and applauding audiences encouraged him to repeat entire movements.

After returning to Vienna, Haydn grew tired of writing symphonies but continued to compose songs, oratorios, string quartets, and even the Austrian national anthem. In 1805 a London newspaper mistakenly printed Haydn's obituary, and England went into a period of mourning. The composer was forced to state that he was still alive, humbly writing, "How can I die now? . . . I have only just begun to understand the wind instruments."[34] In 1809, however, the master did die.

Although Haydn spent most of his life in a prince's palace isolated from the rest of society, his musical contribution is legendary. As Haydn's biographer Ernst Ludwig Gerber wrote in 1790:

> When we speak of Joseph Haydn, we think of one of our greatest men: great in small things and even greater in large; the pride of our age. Always rich and inexhaustible; forever new and surprising, forever noble and great, even when he seems to laugh. He gave to our instrumental music, and in particular to quartets and symphonies, a perfection that never before existed.[35]

Mozart the Child Prodigy

Around 1783, Haydn developed a friendship with the twenty-seven-year-old Mozart, whom he considered one of the greatest composers of the age. In a letter to concert promoter Franz Rotz, Haydn had high praise for the young composer: "If only I could impress Mozart's inimitable works on the soul of every friend of music, and the souls of high personages in particular, as deeply, with the same musical understanding and with the same deep feeling, as I understand and feel them, the nations would vie with each other to possess such a jewel."[36]

Haydn's wish that Mozart could find royal patronage was based on a harsh reality. Even as Mozart was composing immortal works that have remained popular throughout the centuries, he garnered little respect from his employers or the general public. When he was in his twenties, Mozart struggled to survive by giving lessons and selling sheet music of his sonatas. Mozart's dilemma was particularly trou-

Wolfgang Amadeus Mozart was painted as a child playing the pianoforte. Mozart was a child prodigy and toured extensively starting at age six.

bling as he had once been a child star in the concert halls and royal courts of Europe.

Mozart was born on January 27, 1756, and like Bach, Mozart was born into a musical family. His father, Leopold, was a composer and violinist for the respected thirty-eight-piece court orchestra in Salzburg. Leopold was married to Anna Maria Mozart, and the couple had seven children, only two of which survived: the fourth child, a daughter named Maria Anna Walburga Ignatia, called Nannerl; and the seventh and last child, a boy. Leopold believed this child was a miracle because he was so small and weak. They called him Wolfgang. His second name, Amadeus, meant "loved by God" in Latin.

Mozart could plunk out tunes on the piano when he was three, and his ears were so sensitive that loud noises would make him physically ill. The boy also had perfect pitch—the ability to name a note simply by hearing it. At the age of four, he was telling court musicians that their violins were slightly out of tune. By that time, according to Mozart's first biographer Friedrich Schlichtegroll, Mozart could learn a minuet in thirty minutes "and then play it perfectly, cleanly, and with the steadiest rhythm."[37]

Touring Europe

Mozart wrote his first composition, Symphony No. 1, at age six, prompting his father to recognize that the young genius might be able to support the family with his talents. Nannerl, too, was a musical child prodigy, and so Leopold and his two children began an extensive tour of the royal courts, musical academies, and public concerts of Europe playing for imperial ministers, archdukes, emperors, and queens.

To enhance his musical shows, Mozart would perform tricks taught to him by his father, such as playing complicated music on first sight, giving demonstrations of his perfect pitch, and playing a clavier keyboard that was covered by a cloth, so he could not see the keys. As word spread of the young man's talents, the Mozarts were invited to play in England, France, Germany, and elsewhere. During his travels, the young boy met many famous musicians of the day, heard all styles of music from the many regions of the continent, and remembered them for use in his later compositions.

When Mozart traveled to Italy at the age of fourteen, he was inspired to write his first opera, *Mitridate, rè di Ponto*, which was performed in Milan in December 1770. The opera was enthusiastically received, as Leopold wrote in a letter to his wife: "God be praised, the first performance of the Opera . . . took place on the 26th amid general applause. . . . Never in living memory was such curiosity over a first Opera to be seen in Milan as this time."[38]

By 1773 Mozart had written four masses, two long operas, and one short operetta, twelve choral works, and at least thirty symphonies, each about ten minutes long. Music critic Harold C. Schonberg describes the talents of Mozart:

> There was literally nothing in music he could not do better than anybody else. He could write down a complicated piece while thinking out another piece in his head; or he could think out a complete string quartet and then write out the individual parts before making the full score; or he could read perfectly at sight any music placed before him; or he could hear a long piece of music for the first time and immediately write it out, note for note.[39]

"The Most Natural Musician"

Although Mozart was an incredibly gifted composer and musician, by the time he reached his late teens, he was no longer a child prodigy who could attract standing-room-only crowds to his concerts. Unable to find work elsewhere, Mozart took a low-paying job as Kapellmeister for the archbishop of Salzburg in 1773. He continued to compose operas, symphonies, oratorios, quartets, concertos, sonatas, and other works.

During this period, Mozart suffered through the death of his mother and a rocky marriage. At one point, he was so poor he was forced to pawn his belongings. While his life was a shambles, Mozart continued to write joyous, enduring music. From his pen flowed the *Coronation Mass*, the beautiful E-flat Concerto for two pianos, and the equally marvelous Sinfonia Concertante for violin, viola, and orchestra. In addition he received a major commission for the opera *Idomeneo* about the king of ancient Crete who returns home to many problems after fighting the Trojan War.

Tired of working for unappreciative employers, Mozart finally struck out on his own in 1777. He began working as one of the world's first freelance musicians—a job few other less famous composers could manage. His fortunes began to improve as he held performances as a solo virtuoso pianist in concert halls and entertained numbers of rich patrons who enjoyed his musical talents.

In 1782 Mozart wrote the comic opera, *The Abduction from the Seraglio*, about a Spanish nobleman who rescues his lover from a Turkish harem. The characters were dressed in Turkish costumes, considered exotic and exciting at that time, and the opera was an extraordinary success. Working with Italian poet and lyricist Lorenzo Da Ponte, Mozart wrote three more immortal operas between 1786 and 1790: *The Marriage of Figaro, Don Giovanni,* and *Così fan tutte.* The first two were immediate successes when they were performed in Prague, and Mozart achieved the greatest widespread public acclaim of his career.

In 1791, working with actor Emanuel Schikaneder, Mozart wrote yet another comic opera, *The Magic Flute*, a fairy tale about a prince who tries to rescue a maiden. The opera features clever tunes, special musical effects, witches, monsters, and other entertainments that made it a stunning success over the course of one hundred performances.

Soon after writing *The Magic Flute*, Mozart became ill with exhaustion and fever. At one o'clock in the morning on December 5, 1791, Wolfgang Amadeus Mozart died at the age of thirty-six. Although the exact cause of death remains unknown, modern researchers suggest that the composer suffered from kidney failure.

In the years after his death, the world became aware of Mozart's musical genius, realizing that the composer excelled in all forms of classical music. In the short thirty-

An eighteenth-century illustration shows a scene from The Magic Flute. The opera includes crowd pleasing entertainments such as monsters and witches.

DIE ZAUBERFLÖTE.
I. Act.
Tamino. Ach rettet, schützet mich!—

six years of his life, he wrote more than six hundred extraordinary pieces of music and gave the world a legacy of music that many believe is still unsurpassed to this day. By the nineteenth century, it was apparent to many that Mozart was, in the words of Schonberg, "the most perfect, best equipped, and most natural musician the world has ever known."[40]

Beethoven's Wealth of Ideas

Well aware of Mozart's talents and fame, twenty-one-year-old Ludwig van Beethoven planned to travel to Vienna to study with the composer. Unfortunately, Mozart died before Beethoven met him. As a result, Beethoven turned to Haydn for inspiration. As Beethoven's patron Count Waldstein counseled, "You will receive the spirit of Mozart from the hands of Haydn."[41] Whether or not Beethoven ever captured the spirit of Mozart remains a matter of debate among music scholars. Whatever the case, the lives of Mozart and Beethoven followed similar paths and both composers are considered giants of the classical era.

Beethoven was born on December 17, 1770, in the city of Bonn, then a part of the Austrian empire. Like Mozart, Beethoven was from a musical family. His grandfather, also named Ludwig, was the Kapellmeister employed by the elector of Cologne. His father, Johann, was an uncelebrated tenor singer also employed by the elector. Johann, who was a violent alcoholic, desperately wanted his son to be a child prodigy like Mozart. He forced Beethoven to practice for hours. When Beethoven made musical mistakes, his father would beat him around the ears. This seriously damaged Beethoven's ability to hear in later years.

By the time the young Beethoven journeyed to Vienna to take lessons from Haydn, he was a talented, temperamental musician determined to make a name for himself. He played at fashionable private parties where he began improvising—making up the music as he played—which thrilled his wealthy patrons. In fits of musical passion, Beethoven would smash his hands down on the keyboard so hard he would break piano strings. In 1838 Ferdinand Ries, a friend of Beethoven's and his first biographer, wrote about the pianist's improvisational style: "All the artists I ever heard improvise did not come anywhere near the heights reached by Beethoven in his discipline. The wealth of ideas which poured forth, the moods to which he surrendered himself, the variety of interpretation, the complicated challenges which evolved or which he introduced were inexhaustible."[42]

Although Beethoven performed for formally dressed, upper-class audiences, he seldom took care of his own

August Klober painted this portrait of Ludwig van Beethoven in 1818. Beethoven became totally deaf in his later years but continued to write music.

appearance, and his hair was always wild and unruly. His moods changed constantly, and his friends never knew when a chance remark might be taken the wrong way, sending the pianist into fits of rage. While Beethoven was difficult, the nobility flocked to hear his music, and the composer's future looked bright. Compositions flowed from him, and he toured often, giving concerts in Prague, at the royal court of Prussia in Berlin, and in other important European cities.

Beethoven's Torment

By the time Beethoven turned thirty, he was losing his hearing. Beethoven writes of this experience in a letter to his friend Franz Wegeler:

> [My] ears whistle and buzz continually day and night. I can say I am living a wretched life; for two years I have avoided almost all social gatherings because it is impossible for me to say to people: "I am deaf." If I belonged to any other profession it would be easier, but in my profession it is an awful state, the more since my enemies, who are not a few, what would they say? In order to give you an idea of this singular deafness of mine I must tell you that in the theatre I must get very close to the orchestra in order to understand the actor. If I am a little distant I do not hear the high tones of the instruments, singers, and if I be but a little farther away I do not hear at all . . . . Heaven knows what will happen to me. . . . I have often cursed my existence . . . there will be moments in my life when I am the unhappiest of God's creatures.

Quoted in Alexander Thayer. *The Life of Ludwig van Beethoven, Vol. 1*. Ann Arbor: UMI, 1989, p. 300.

The Heroic Style

By 1800, Beethoven was in his prime. He wrote the famous *Pathétique* sonata, five piano sonatas, three violin sonatas, two cello sonatas, the Trio in B-flat Major, six string quartets, a quintet, chamber music, and songs including the famous "Adelaide."

The year 1800 also marked the first performance of Beethoven's Symphony No. 1. In 1801 Beethoven wrote the music for the ballet *The Creatures of Prometheus*, which was performed many times in Vienna. Among his other works that year were the famous pieces known as *The Funeral March* (Piano Sonata Opus 26) and the *Moonlight Sonata* (Piano Sonata Opus 27).

While creating enduring works of music, Beethoven began to lose his hearing when he was around thirty years old. Despite this handicap, the composer carried on, writing symphonies in what has been called "the heroic style" for their timeless and dramatic quality. As Mann writes: "Beethoven wanted his audience to regard music not as the entertainment accepted by earlier audiences, but as some sort of sermon about the godlike nature of man."[43]

Beethoven's third through eighth symphonies are triumphant displays of the composer's genius, written ironically, when he was almost completely deaf. Sherman and Seldon describe Beethoven's work during this time: "Beethoven embarked on a revolutionary path. From here on, he would experiment with new forms even as he was expanding the old ones, invent his own musical parameters, produce works on a vast and heroic scale, and ultimately shatter existing preconceptions about the expressive potential of music altogether."[44]

Although he spent most of the later years of his life in self-imposed isolation, Beethoven continued to write. While almost totally deaf, he could hear the vibrations of the notes by laying his head on the piano. When he finally died at the age of fifty-six, the composer's death was as dramatic as his music.

At 5:45 P.M. on March 26, 1827, a large clap of thunder rocked Vienna, and a flash of lightning filled the room where Beethoven was lying sick and unconscious. Fellow composer Anselm Hüttenbrenner wrote, "After this unexpected phenomenon of nature . . . Beethoven opened his eyes, lifted his right hand and looked up several seconds with his fist clenched and a very serious, threatening expression. . . . When he let the raised hand sink to the bed, his eyes closed half-way. . . . Not another breath, not another heartbeat more!"[45]

Several days later, his funeral procession through the streets of Vienna attracted twenty thousand people. They came to pay their respects to the man who would someday be recognized as one of the greatest musical geniuses of the nineteenth century.

While the extraordinary symphonic gifts of Haydn, Mozart, and Beethoven dominated the classical era, they were joined by other men who also made lasting contributions. Yet, it was the opening "Da-da-da-dummmm" chords of Beethoven's Fifth Symphony and the melodies of Mozart's *The Magic Flute* that continue to define the classical period nearly two centuries later.

CHAPTER 4

The Romantic Era

In late 1823, the German composer Carl Maria von Weber visited the apartment of Ludwig van Beethoven in Vienna. Weber described the room as dreary and "in the greatest disorder: music, money, clothes, lay on the floor, linen in a heap on the unclean bed, the open grand piano was covered in thick dust, and broken coffee-cups lay on the table."[46] Beethoven, who was fifty-three at the time, was struggling financially—and completely deaf. Despite the composer's circumstances, he was hard at work creating one of the most joyous, exhilarating, and influential compositions in music history: Symphony No. 9, or simply Beethoven's Ninth.

When the Ninth was performed at Vienna's Kärntnertor Theater on May 7, 1824, Beethoven stood center stage while another man conducted. Because of his hearing loss, Beethoven was deaf to the one-hundred-piece orchestra playing the complex and stirring Ninth. After the grand finale, "Ode to Joy," performed by a chorus of more than ninety singers, the audience erupted in thunderous applause. Beethoven, still poring over his sheet music with his back to the audience, was unaware of the ovation.

While Beethoven is recognized as one of the titans of classical music, the Ninth is credited with moving Western music into a new period called the romantic era. This period in mu-

sic lasted from about 1810 to 1900. During this time, romantic composers abandoned what they considered to be the dry
formal styles of great masters. Inspired by earth-changing
events such as the American and French revolutions, a
new generation of composers experimented with innovative musical ideas that were also considered revolutionary.

Moody and Expressive

The term *romanticism* was first used to describe the literary
style of the late 1700s. The founding author of the movement was Johann Wolfgang von Goethe, whose 1774 book
Faust exemplified the romantic style. The emotional, expressive, and moody story is about a man who sold his soul
to the devil in trade for immortality and the love of an un-
obtainable woman.

Romantic composers often created music based on books,
poems, or plays, and several operas were based on *Faust*.
Other operas of the era drew from supernatural medieval
tales filled with evil spirits, witches, and soul-snatching demons. Beethoven was also inspired by the romantic poets.
He had first contemplated setting the romantic philosopher
Friedrich Schiller's poem "Ode to Joy" to music in 1790.
When he finally did so in the 1820s, the rest of the Ninth
flowed from Schiller's ode. When it was finally completed,
the Ninth inspired a new generation of romantics to create
music that invoked fear, awe, horror, and, sometimes, feelings of joyous liberation.

Romantic music also drew from real world political
events. After Napoleon became the emperor of France in
1804, he attempted to conquer all of Europe. The Napoleonic
Wars, which lasted until 1815, created misery across the
continent. When Napoleon was defeated, there was a rising
tide of nationalism in European countries. People became
very devoted, sometimes fanatically so, to the cultures and
accomplishments of their homelands. This was reflected
in the music of the romantic era, as Robert Sherman and
Philip Seldon write:

> [There was a] turn toward works that evoked pride in
> the creator's homeland. Composers in the Romantic era

took special note of traditions in their native countries, giving symphonic life to country folk tunes and rustic dance rhythms, painting tonal landscapes of rivers, mountains, and castles, bringing national poetry and other literary works to bear on their musical instincts. Thus we find classical pieces deriving from local legends . . . nature sketches . . . or historical personages.[47]

The Contrasting Characteristics of Romantic and Classical Music

Music journalist Dhun H. Sethna describes the differences between the classical and romantic music styles:

[Classical and Romantic relate] to the two basic instincts of human nature: on the one hand, the need to control and moderate the emotions and, on the other, to express an . . . emotional longing for the forbidden, the unknown and the unattainable. [Where] the Classical aroused [feelings of rest] and serenity, the . . . Romantic suggested restlessness and disorder. Eternal longing, regret for the lost happiness of childhood, or [discontent] gnawed at the soul and formed the ingredients of the Romantic spirit. . . . [Where] the Classical had found inspiration in the gods and heroes of ancient Greece, the Romantics discovered the Dark Ages . . . fairy tales and medieval sagas, folk dances and nationalism. Here were the great themes of the triumph of good over evil, of God and nature, of life and death and man's destiny, and of the struggle for freedom. In its music it found expression in the great heaven storming climaxes, the violent contrasts between deafening loudness and a whispering softness, and in [touching] melodies.

Dhun H. Sethna. *Classical Music for Everybody.* Sierra Madre, CA: Fitzwilliam, 1997, p. 117.

Telling Stories Through Sound

The musical celebration of folktales, national pride, and natural wonders defines the romantic era. With composers inspired by literature and the visual arts, the period was a time of glorifying the fantastic, the bizarre, the beautiful, the emotional, and the creative. This allowed composers the freedom to put aside formal structures of the past and explore unique approaches to music. They might utilize short segments of dissonant chord progressions or rely on a long drawn-out solo by a distinctive sounding instrument, even if it interrupted the natural flow of the symphony.

Another hallmark of the romantic era involved the pairing of music and words. For example, Goethe was a musician who created poetry specifically written to be set to music. Beethoven greatly admired Goethe and set several of his poems to song. This mix is called *lieder* (pronounced leeder) in German. Franz Schubert was the leader of the lied, writing an incredible 145 songs in the eighteenth year of his life. Before his untimely death at the age of thirty-one, Schubert wrote more than six hundred lieder, seventy of them based on the poems of Goethe.

Schubert's moody lieder used orchestral instrument to create sounds like babbling brooks and gathering storm clouds. These unique pieces inspired some romantic composers to do away with the words altogether and attempt to tell stories with instruments alone. These are called *tone poems*, or symphonic poems—orchestral works based on literature that tell an often complicated tale through music. These pieces might inspire listeners to imagine fields, forests, or other landscapes or think of specific characters from a novel or poem. The most complex tone poems try to convert complete stories to musical sounds.

The Contradictions of Schumann

One of the most gifted creators of tone poems was Robert Schumann, born in Saxony in 1810. Schumann learned to play the piano as soon as he was tall enough to reach the keys. By the age of eleven, he was directing his school band. As he grew older, Schumann fell in love with literature and wrote poems, stories, and even several novels, all of which remained unfinished.

After penning his first musical compositions in the early 1830s, Schumann became editor-in-chief of the magazine *New Journal of Music*, a position he held from 1834 to 1844. The journal was a leading advocate of romantic music, and Schumann wrote satirical essays for the magazine. According to composer Marion Bauer and historian Ethel Peyser, one Schumann story was about a fictional group of musicians who "were fighting against the musical Philistines. It was a struggle of a new order against the old; of the ultra-modern Romanticism against the decadent Classicism; of the youthful, subjective, and emotional against the artificial and [dull]."[48] In his essays, Schumann often sang the praises of romantic geniuses such as Frédéric Chopin, Johannes Brahms, and Schubert, who were relatively unknown at that time.

In addition to his magazine work, Schumann published dozens of piano compositions. These song cycles such as "Vienna Carnival Pranks," "Fantasy Pieces," and "Scenes from Childhood," are meant to evoke particular images in the listener's mind. As music professor Donald J. Grout and romantic music authority Claude V. Palisca write,

> Schumann intended his music not only to be considered as patterns of sound, but in some manner to suggest [poetic fantasies]. His music embodies . . . the depths . . . and tensions of the Romantic spirit; it is by turns [passionate] and dreamy, vehement and visionary, whimsical and learned.[49]

Schumann's passionate work reached a pinnacle in 1840 when, his spirits cheered by marriage, the composer wrote 138 lieder in what he called a single "year of song."[50] Some of these titles, "You Are Like a Flower," "A Poet's Love," "In the Beautiful Month of May," and "A Woman's Love and Life," demonstrate the composer's contented mental state at the time. For the next several years Schumann specialized in specific forms. For instance, in 1841 he wrote only orchestral music, specifically four symphonies; in 1842 it was chamber music that included three string quartets, a piano quartet, and a piano quintet.

A stereoscope photograph from 1850 shows Robert Schumann and his wife, Clara. Clara was a child prodigy and toured to support her family after her husband's death.

Unfortunately the romantic composer's mental health began to imitate romantic literature as he became moody, depressed, and suffered from loss of memory. Like the story of an opera, Schumann began to hear voices in his head. According to Harold C. Schonberg: "In early 1852, he went through an entire week during which he said that angels were dictating music to him while devils in the form of tigers and hyenas were threatening him with Hell."[51] In February of that year Schumann threw himself into the Rhine River. Although he did not die, his musical voice was silenced as he spent the last few years of his life in a mental institution. He died at the age of forty-six.

After Schumann's death, his wife, Clara Schumann, who was a virtuoso pianist, continued to play his music. Clara was a child prodigy who had been recognized for her talents at age twelve. After Schumann's passing, Clara supported herself and her eight children by giving recitals throughout Europe. During this era, the prolific pianist Fanny Mendelssohn, who died in 1847, was one of the only

Fanny Mendelssohn Plays in a Man's World

During the romantic era, refined young women were forbidden to enter into the "man's world" of composing music. But Fanny Mendelssohn, sister of composer Felix Mendelssohn, was one of the few nineteenth-century women recognized for her musical talents.

Mendelssohn's parents were wealthy, and Fanny was provided with the finest education. Both Felix and Fanny showed musical talent and performed public recitals together when they were teenagers. However, when Fanny turned fourteen in 1819, her father wrote her a letter dismissing her dreams: "Perhaps music will be his [Felix's] profession, whereas for you it can and must be an ornament, and never the fundamental base-line of your existence."

Denied the right to practice her talents, Fanny married a respectable gentleman and attempted to forget about writing music. She became depressed, however, when she could not compose. When she attempted to publish some of her work, Felix talked her out of it. In 1845, at the age of forty, Fanny finally went against her brother's wishes and published some of her 486 pieces of music, which were well received by critics. Unfortunately, she died suddenly two years later. Wracked by guilt, Felix had more of her work published before he died only six months later.

Quoted in Françoise Tillard. *Fanny Mendelssohn*. Portland, OR: Amadeus, 1992, p. 68.

well-known female composers. Playing her own pieces including concertos, lieder, and other piano music, Clara Schumann took her place next to Mendelssohn, earning the nickname "Queen of the Piano." In addition to playing her own compositions, Schumann tirelessly promoted her husband's work. Because of her efforts, the music of both Clara and Robert Schumann remains popular today.

The Vivid Stories of Berlioz

Schumann based many of his pieces on poems meant to evoke specific feelings in the listener, such as the exhilaration of a fresh spring day in the song "In the Beautiful Month of May." Other romantic composers promoted more ambitious ideas and wrote texts of words or *programs* to be read by the audience before the music was played. These programs contained detailed descriptions of stories, objects, or scenery the composer was attempting to convey with pieces called *program music*.

The composer at the forefront of the program music movement is Hector Berlioz. Born to a wealthy family near Grenoble, France, in 1803, Berlioz chose to forsake a fortune in order to study theater and singing. He also learned to play guitar, flute, and piano. Although Berlioz had no technical training and was not a child prodigy, he had an extremely active imagination that allowed him to create grand compositions of timeless quality.

However strong his imagination might have been, Berlioz, cut off from his family fortune, struggled for years to prove himself to an indifferent public. All the while, he suffered through a debilitating bout of unrequited love for an Irish actress named Henrietta Smithson. With his life unfolding like a romantic opera, Berlioz channeled his emotional distress into a grand epic. His 1830 masterpiece of program music called *Symphonie Fantastique* is passionate and dramatic, featuring musical descriptions of pastoral beauty and the tortured dreams of an opium addict, which are played out in a witches' Sabbath. Berlioz, who was an opium addict himself, finishes *Symphonie Fantastique* with a vision of his own execution.

Berlioz gave the symphony the subtitle "Episode in the Life of an Artist" to ensure listeners understood the music was autobiographical. In the accompanying program, he describes the need for written words: "The program should be regarded in the same way as the spoken words of an opera, serving to introduce the musical numbers by describing the situation that evokes the particular mood and expressive character of each."[52]

What Berlioz's program clarifies in black and white, his music expresses in a wide range of cleverly written sounds meant to soothe, startle, frighten, and even shock the listener. Flutes imitate bird calls, harps create a peaceful mood, timpani drums echo distant thunder, clarinets shriek like wicked demons, guttural trombones spit out a march to the gallows, and violinists hit their strings with the wooden part of their bows to imitate skeletons rattling their bones.

Berlioz won some respect for his experimental symphony, but he also attracted severe criticism for producing what

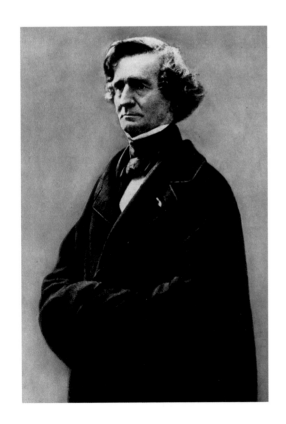

The composer Hector Berlioz was photographed by the artist Nadar around 1860. Berlioz's musical experimentations were decades ahead of his time.

some critics simply considered harsh noise. Despite the stinging words of the critics, the composer's emotionally turbulent life continued to inspire music on a grand scale. As Berlioz became more dedicated to proving his worth as a composer, he began to write pieces for huge orchestras. Berlioz hired 150 people to play the *Symphonie Fantastique*, an effort considered outrageous at that time. Yet, even this was not enough for the composer who envisioned the ideal orchestra as having 467 musicians accompanied by a chorus of 360 singers. This orchestra would include thirty harps, an equal number of pianos, 242 violins, and a range of unusual percussion instruments unheard of in the nineteenth century.

Berlioz never assembled his fantasy orchestra. While he was revered for his visionary ideas by some—and severely

The Macabre Life of an Artist

Hector Berlioz wrote Symphonie Fantastique *about his deep love for the Irish actress Henrietta Smithson. Composer Marion Bauer and historian Ethel Peyser describe Berlioz's symphony:*

> [*Symphonie Fantastique* was] written by the young composer as a result of his infatuation with Henrietta Smithson. It describes the drug-laden amorous dreams of a young musician who muses with alternate hope and despair upon the thought of his beloved. The five movements are entitled: "Reveries, Passions," a free form movement discontinues in motion in which the lover examines his "weariness of soul" and "volcanic love"; "A Ball," in the form of an elegant French waltz, wherein the lover visualizes his beloved at a brilliant [gala]; "Scene in the Country," a [rustic musical poem] . . . in which the artist broods and wonders about her, as shepherds pipe and thunder rumbles in the distance; "March to the Gallows," in which the lover dreams he has killed his loved one and is condemned to death by guillotine (depicted with extreme realism); "Dream of a Witches' Sabbath," [a fantasy] . . . full of "unearthly sounds, groans, shrieks of laughter, distant cries," carried into satire.

Marion Bauer and Ethel Peyser. *Music Through the Ages.* New York: G.P. Putnam's Sons, 1967, pp. 452–453.

condemned by others—he was the first to propose such ideas that later became accepted features of symphonies and orchestras. Decades ahead of his time, Hector Berlioz was the epitome of romantic experimentation.

Lisztomania

While Berlioz was criticized for his romantic excesses, Hungarian-born pianist Franz Liszt was one of the biggest

Pianist and composer Franz Liszt was one of the most popular musicians of his time.

stars of his day. Like other romantic composers, Liszt had a deep affinity for literature. He took this love and blended it with a technical wizardry on the keyboard that few have matched.

Liszt loved to experiment with sounds in his pieces, and he used a dramatic and fiery style to perform his works. He studied the folk music of his native land and popularized the song style known as *rhapsody* that incorporates the improvised melodies, fast-paced rhythms, and sentimental passions of Hungarian Gypsy music. He combined these with a flair for performance that created hysterical adoration known as Lisztomania, similar to the attention received by modern rock stars. Journalist David Pogue and music director Scott Speck describe Liszt's playing style:

[While] touring all across Europe to sold-out concert halls . . . [Liszt turned his] performances into rockin' road shows: removing a trademark pair of white gloves with a flourish just before playing, insisting on a backup piano onstage in case he broke strings with his violent crashes on the keyboard, and showing off his memorization skills by dramatically tossing the sheet music over his shoulder before beginning to play. . . . Of course, his fans went wild. So many people wrote to him asking for a lock of his hair that he had to get a dog—he cut off little pieces of fur whenever necessary. *Lisztomania* . . . was out of control.[53]

In addition to writing sixteen Hungarian rhapsodies, Liszt created symphonic poems to Shakespeare's *Hamlet,* Goethe's *Faust,* and Dante's *Divine Comedy.* He also wrote dozens of solo piano pieces that only the most technically skilled musicians can play.

Romantic Italian Opera

While Liszt's impressive performances were seen by large audiences, nothing in the nineteenth century offered as grand a spectacle as opera. Stage productions often featured dozens of moving pieces of scenery, smoke machines, and singers in harnesses flying about the stage on wires controlled from above. These grand productions attracted society's most powerful men and women showing off the latest fashions and hair styles.

Aside from its social context, nineteenth-century opera was the perfect romantic synthesis of overwrought emotion, majestic scenes of nature, and supernatural freakishness. This so called "union of the arts" according to Bauer and Peyser, combined "music, drama, visual effects, dancing, miming and message."[54]

While the union of the arts was popular throughout Europe, there were two main schools of opera: the Italian and the German-Austrian. The master of Italian opera was Gioacchino Rossini, born in 1792. Rossini was so prolific that he was able to write thirty-eight operas by the time he was thirty-seven years old. In 1823 alone, twenty-three of his operas were in production somewhere in Europe. Although the composer barely wrote anything in the last half of his life, his works such as *Otello, Cinderella, The Thieving Magpie, William Tell,* and *The Barber of Seville,* strongly influenced romantic opera composers for the rest of the century.

The Operas of Verdi

A 2010 production of Giuseppe Verdi's opera Aïda *is performed in front of the Sphinx in Giza, Egypt. Verdi's operas remain popular and are performed around the world.*

Giuseppe Verdi was born in 1813, a time when Rossini was writing about five operas a year. Although he would not match Rossini's output, Verdi is considered one of the greatest composers of nineteenth-century Italian opera.

Verdi was the son of a poor tavern keeper in Parma, Italy, an area shattered by political upheaval, revolution, and war. Unlike many composers who were born to wealth or hailed from musical families, Verdi was of the peasant class. However, his musical talents allowed him to marry a woman of wealth, and she helped stage his first opera, *Oberto,* in

1839. Verdi's second opera, the 1842 *Nabucco*, based on the life of ancient Babylonian king Nebuchadnezzar, made him a star in Italy. While the music may sound less than spectacular to modern ears, when the opera debuted, an unnamed critic wrote that the music was "so new, was so unknown, the style so rapid, so unusual, that everybody was amazed."[55]

As Verdi's fame spread across Europe, he reached his peak in 1853, composing both *Il Trovatore* (*The Troubadour*) and *La Traviata* (*The Lost Lady*) in a single year. Along with his 1851 opera *Rigoletto*, based on a story by French poet and novelist Victor Hugo, this trio of Verdi productions was performed annually in the opera houses of Paris, London, Rome, and Venice. In 1871 Verdi wrote the masterpiece *Aïda*, commissioned by the Egyptian government for the opening of the Suez Canal.

Verdi's operatic works of genius remain popular today. More than a century after his death in 1901, Verdi's operas are in continual production, and his music has enriched and inspired the lives of millions of fans.

Wagner's Influential Opera

Verdi was the indisputable king of nineteenth-century Italian opera, but he had an archrival in composer Richard Wagner, the undisputed king of German-Austrian opera. Born in Leipzig, Germany in 1813, Wagner is called "the greatest Romanticist of all"[56] by Bauer and Peyser. Because of his affinity for composing opera, he is considered the German version of Verdi.

Like many other romantic composers, Wagner was fascinated by literature as a young man and began writing music to literary themes in his teens. Wagner's first successful opera, the 1842 *Rienzi*, helped the composer land a job as the director of opera in Dresden. Wagner began writing his own *librettos*, or stories, to accompany his operas, something few composers ever attempted. By the end of the 1840s, Wagner was working on a colossal cycle of four music dramas known as *Der Ring des Nibelungen* (*The Ring of the Nibelung*), which included the now-famous *Das Rheingold*

Bryn Terfel and Katarina Dalayman perform in a production of Die Walküre—the second of the four operas of The Ring of the Nibelung—in 2012. Some consider Richard Wagner's Ring Cycle one of the greatest achievements of Western culture.

(The Rhine Gold), Die Walküre (The Valkyrie), Siegfried, and Die Götterdämmerung (The Twilight of the Gods). This monumental undertaking consumed twenty-two years of Wagner's life. This cycle of operas, which Stanley Sadie and Alison Latham call the "greatest achievements of Western culture,"[57] is based on ancient tales of gods, giants, humans, and dwarves called Nibelungs. The symbolism behind the stories was meant to relate to real-world political events such as the industrialization of society and the growth of socialism in Europe.

Wagner influenced nineteenth century music in several areas: He brought German opera to its peak as Verdi had done with Italian opera. He also created a new form called music drama, best demonstrated in the 1865 *Tristan und*

Isolde that alternates scenes of action with dialogue and a narrative monologue. In addition to his musical works, Wagner wrote extensively about nineteenth-century politics and culture, throwing his support behind the 1848 revolution in Germany with fiery words of propaganda. Unfortunately, the composer was extremely anti-Semitic, and his anti-Jewish writings inspired Adolf Hitler and the Nazis in the twentieth century. Although this has left Wagner despised by some modern critics, his musical drama was unequaled in the romantic era. As Sadie and Latham write:

> As no one had done before, [Wagner] changed opera— not just opera, but music itself. Not just music, but indeed art: the impact of this man, his creations and his thought, left the world a different place. He arouses men's passions, intellectual and emotional, as no artist had done before, nor any since. . . . He has been hailed as a high priest of a thousand philosophies. . . . His music is hated as much as it is worshipped. The only issue beyond dispute is his greatness.[58]

The Experimental Age

As the works of Wagner demonstrate, the romantic era was a time of burgeoning creativity when composers attempted to portray real-life events symbolically through music. By using styles such as lieder, tone poems, and program symphonies, music and literature were brought together as never before.

During an age of wars and revolution, romantic composers felt free to make music that was at times violent and macabre. In some of the chaotic pieces of Berlioz, the music almost borders on madness. Despite the controversies, the works of romantic composers stand as monuments to an age when the untried and experimental were allowed to flourish in a world hungry for the new.

CHAPTER 5

The Musical Art of the Modern Era

Classical composers have long drawn inspiration from the artists of their times. After the century-long romantic era ended in the 1860s, impressionist painters like Claude Monet and Pierre-Auguste Renoir rejected the dark, frightful subject matter of the romantics. Instead of painting dark mythical monsters and brooding nature scenes, impressionist artists created soft, pastel works with indistinct blurred outlines. This provided the artist's impression of a scene, rather than a concrete image. Impressionist paintings appear to be created on the spur of the moment, with bright colors, giving the paintings an unusual radiance.

Debussy's Colorful Impressions

The leading composer inspired by impressionism was Claude Debussy, born in 1862. Like impressionist artists, Debussy worked from a palette of bright musical colors that painted vivid musical pictures of peaceful summer days and serene moonlit forests. The titles of his major compositions, written in the 1890s and early 1900s, read like the names of impressionist paintings: *Clouds, Festivals, The Island of Joy, Reflections in the Water, Prelude to the Afternoon of a Faun,* and *The Sea.*

Like the impressionist painters, Debussy's work was initially considered radical, and critics claimed that his music was vague and indefinable. He was later regarded as one of the most influential composers of the twentieth century. Music journalist Mark Prendergast explains, "[His] strange floating and escaping harmonies and his grasp of instrumental timbre . . . earned him the title 'Father of Modern Music'. Certainly, the high points of the twentieth-century electronic music, like Pink Floyd's *Dark Side of the Moon*, were first envisaged in Debussy's ample imagination."[59] Debussy put it more simply, stating: "I am more and more convinced . . . that music by its very nature, is something that cannot be cast in a traditional and fixed form. It is made up of colors and rhythms."[60]

Mahler Screams

Gustav Mahler was born in 1860 and worked during the late nineteenth and early twentieth centuries. Unlike Debussy, who created pleasant sounds of musical impressionism, Mahler's music was inspired by the expressionist painters who followed the impressionists. Expressionists used bold swipes of bright colors to highlight life's greatest fears and deepest anxieties. *The Scream* by Norwegian painter Edvard Munch is the most widely recognized expressionist painting. It depicts a skeletal figure with his mouth wide open and his hands covering his ears under a sky filled with a swirling turmoil of orange, red, and aqua green. The tortured figure in the painting could easily be seen as a caricature of Mahler.

As a child, Mahler's family life was wracked with grief: of the twelve children born to his parents, only six survived infancy. Mahler's father abused his mother, and during one particularly violent episode young Gustav heard a street musician playing a happy drinking song. Later in life, Mahler came to realize that he associated joyful music with great sorrow. In another incident, Mahler's daughter died of scarlet fever several months after he wrote a series of pieces called *Songs on the Death of Children*. This left the composer wracked with guilt. David Pogue and Scott Speck describe

A 1935 painting by Max Oppenheimer shows Gustav Mahler conducting the Vienna Philharmonic Orchestra. Mahler's music was inspired by the expressionist movement.

how Mahler's personal grief affected his work: "[His] music is full of . . . instruments screaming at the extremes of their range; moments of ethereal beauty, rage and torment, desolation, or triumph."[61]

As a hard-driving perfectionist, Mahler's compositions took him years to finish. For example, his First Symphony in D took more than a decade to complete. During this time, Mahler wrote protracted symphonies, some that stretched to more than an hour in length, with up to six movements. His subject matter was deep—his Third Symphony, according to the program, is nothing less than "an ascent through the realms of existence."[62]

To perform his works, Mahler needed extremely large orchestras. His 1907 Eighth Symphony in E Flat is called *Symphony of a Thousand*, according to Marion Bauer and Ethel Peyser, because "it is scored for two large mixed choruses, a boys' chorus, eight soloists, and an orchestra of 120, and lasts more than two hours."[63] Mahler also pioneered the concept of changing keys several times in one symphony. According to William Mann, Mahler "took tonal music to limits where it is sometimes impossible to state what key a symphony by him is 'in'. The fourth symphony, for example, begins in G major . . . and ends in E major . . . [an indication] that the music travels from one point to another without having a return ticket, so to speak."[64] At times Mahler experimented with almost painfully off-key chords, such as the nine-note dissonant shriek at the apex of the first movement in his Tenth Symphony.

Mahler wrote pieces based on his search for the meaning of life. In doing so, he transformed musical rules about key, harmony, and tempo established as far back as the tenth century. While Mahler's dedication to pushing musical boundaries took precedence over what the average audience might appreciate, he explored new avenues of musical experimentation and inspired many composers who followed in the modern era.

Igor Stravinsky conducts a concert in 1968. His work with dissonant harmonies was influential among twentieth-century composers.

Stravinsky's Riots of Spring

Igor Stravinsky jokingly referred to Mahler as *Malheur*, the French word for misfortune. Whatever the Russian-born Stravinsky thought of his colleague, there is little doubt that the two men shared similar musical inspirations. Like Mahler, Stravinsky scored his works such as the ballets *The Firebird* (1910) and *Petrushka* (1911) for large orchestras. Stravinsky was also fond of expressionist-style pounding chords and dissonant harmonies. His *The Rite of Spring* literally caused riots when it debuted in Paris in 1913. The crowd felt that Stravinsky's groundbreaking composition was actually a blasphemous effort to destroy music. Dissonance—music written with combinations of notes that sound off-key but are meant to suggest unrelieved tension—would come to be a guiding force among the

The Rite of Spring Causes a Riot

When composer Igor Stravinsky's ballet The Rite of Spring *debuted in Paris on May 28, 1913, the intense, dissonant, rhythmic music and pagan dances shocked the public. The audience responded to the music with whistles and catcalls. Fistfights broke out in the aisles before police arrived to quell the riot. In his 1936 autobiography, Stravinsky describes the scene:*

> I left the auditorium [to stand in the wings] at the first bars of the prelude, which had at once evoked derisive laughter. I was disgusted. These demonstrations, at first isolated, soon became general, provoking counter-demonstrations and very quickly developing into a terrific uproar. During the whole performance I was at Nijinsky's [the choreographer's] side in the wings. . . . He was standing on a chair, screaming . . . [out the beat] to keep time. Naturally, the poor dancers could hear nothing by reason of the row in the auditorium and the sound of their own dance steps. I had to hold Nijinsky [back], for he was furious, and ready to dash on stage at any moment and create a scandal. Diaghilev [the producer] kept ordering the electricians to turn the lights on or off, hoping in that way to put a stop to the noise.

Igor Stravinsky. *An Autobiography*. New York: W.W. Norton, 1998, p. 47.

leading composers of the twentieth century. Stravinsky tried to explain the importance of dissonance in composition when paired with its musical opposite, consonance:

Consonance, says the dictionary, is the combination of several tones into a harmonic unit. Dissonance results from the deranging of this harmony by the addition of tones foreign to it. . . . Ever since it appeared in our vocabulary, the word "dissonance" has carried with it a certain odor of sinfulness. Let us light our lantern: in textbook language, dissonance is an element of transition, a complex or interval of tones that is not complete in itself and that must be resolved to the ear's satisfaction into a perfect consonance.[65]

Schoenberg's Violent Expression

While Stravinsky's music might have been considered controversial at the time, it sounded harmonious when compared to Arnold Schoenberg's discordant twelve-tone expressionist compositions. Schoenberg went beyond Mahler's tendency to write symphonies in several keys; he abandoned musical keys altogether. His music was labeled *atonal*. As a radical departure from traditional music, atonal music has no fixed key and creates dissonant music, often harsh and unfamiliar to the ear.

Born in Vienna in 1874, Schoenberg did not come from a musical family. Although he played the violin at eight, he did not formally study music until he was almost eighteen. Schoenberg began experimenting with music almost as soon as he began composing it at the age of twenty. A symphonic poem he wrote in 1899 was the first work in which a composer ever used a trombone *glissando*—a rapid slide through a series of consecutive notes.

Schoenberg began composing increasingly complicated works. His *Songs of Gurre*, written between 1901 and 1911, is so intricate, the composer required extra-long music to write it down. It calls for a huge orchestra, and as Donald J. Grout and Claude V. Palisca write, "Schoenberg outdid even Mahler . . . in size and complexity of the score and Wagner in [the] violence of expression."[66]

For his 1912 piece *Moonstruck Pierrot*, Schoenberg created a new style of music. The twenty songs were written in what is called in German *sprechstimme*, or "speech voice." This is described by Robert Sherman and Philip Seldon as "a gliding method of vocal performance midway between speech and song, the singer touching a note but not sustaining it. It produces an eerie effect, perfect for the work's graphic portrayal of creeping madness."[67]

The Twelve-Tone Scale

Schoenberg began experimenting with atonal music in the 1910s but was unhappy with the results. He felt the compositions, which lacked a unifying key, did not have an organized form. Around 1924, to add structure to his pieces, Schoenberg invented *serial music*, or twelve-tone music. This style is based on a series of twelve notes. In Schoenberg's twelve-tone system there are no fixed keys, but each note in a scale (C, C#, D, D#, E, F, F#, G, G#, A, A#, and B) is equally important. Melodies are replaced by the *tone row*, in which each of the twelve notes has to be played once before being repeated. That is, once a note is played, the other eleven have to be presented before the original note can be played again. Compositions consist of sets, or series, of these twelve-note rows. A row might be played backwards, forwards, or by turning the sheet music upside down. Although this method sounds simplistic, mathematicians have calculated that there are a possible 479 million combinations for a twelve-tone row.

Known as serial music, or serialism, this jarring dissonant concept was quite controversial and panned by critics and the general public alike. In fact, Schoenberg was forced to found a private organization, called the Society for Private Musical Performances, so he could play his music. According to Sherman and Seldon, the society excluded the "razor-tongued critics and insult-screaming listeners who had made a shamble of so many open concerts."[68]

Schoenberg, who was Jewish, was forced to flee the vicious persecution of Nazi Germany in the 1930s. He eventually took a post teaching at the University of California, Los Angeles (UCLA), where he lived until his death in 1951. While his music was admired by many composers, the strange-sounding and difficult-to-understand twelve-tone system was intensely disliked by the concert-going public and, therefore, seldom performed.

Alban Berg and Anton von Webern

Despite the fact that most people could not stand to listen to his music, Schoenberg had many musical disciples in the modern era. Alban Berg and Anton von Webern were among those who devoted themselves to Schoenberg's twelve-tone system. The music composed by these men, however, differs from that of their mentor. According to Grout and Palisca, Berg "invested the technique with such a warmth of Romantic feeling that his music is more readily accessible than that of many twelve-tone composers."[69] Berg even used the system to write two expressionistic operas: *Wozzeck* and *Lulu*.

Webern, on the other hand, used Schoenberg's twelve-tone system to create works reminiscent of an earlier era, giving the music an almost classical sound. His pieces are also short. For example, the movements of his 1913 Five Pieces for Orchestra, Opus 10, are thirty-six to forty-nine seconds in length, while larger works, such as the 1938 String Quartet, are only nine minutes long.

Schoenberg, Berg, and Webern oversaw the dissolution of a musical system that had been in place for centuries, beginning with Bach in the 1600s. Twelve-tone music, while shunned by the public, was accepted as a valid system by composers by the 1950s.

The Music of the Avant-Garde

Although the general public did not support twelve-tone music, the style was embraced by a group of young composers who gathered in Darmstadt, Germany, after World War II. This group, known as the *avant-garde*, studied the music of Webern and took it to the next level. Avant-garde is a term originated by painters who created pieces that were highly original, unconventional, innovative, and experimental.

In the post–World War II era, painter Jackson Pollock was considered an avant-garde artist because he produced drip paintings from globs, dribbles, and splashes of colored paints. Like Pollock, avant-garde composers refused to follow traditional rules or established methods. According to Grout and Palisca: "[Every] composer worked independently, striking out in new directions, cultivating his own language, his own style, his own special techniques. There was no allegiance to one consistent body of principles, no well-defined 'common practice'" as in the eighteenth and nineteenth centuries.[70]

The avant-garde composers at Darmstadt strongly influenced classical music in the second half of the twentieth century by creating a style known as *total serialism*. This music lacks tonality, melody, rhythm, and harmony—elements that are contained in almost all previous classical pieces. In a complex continuation of Schoenberg's twelve-tone system, all other aspects of a piece are placed in a repetitive row. These serialized elements include note duration, instrument timbre, length of silences, and even volume. The resulting music is *athematic*, or without a guiding theme. There is no sense of melody, rhythm, or harmony. Unlike earlier classical works since the time of Haydn and Mozart, the pieces do not progress to a general climax at the end. As Grout and Palisca explain:

> [One] was aware only of successive, unrepeated, and unpredictable musical "events." Such events might take the form of . . . "points" of sound—color, melody, rhythm—intertwining, dissolving into one another in an apparently random fashion. Of course, when a work was well constructed . . . [the sound would] form a logical pattern, but it might be a very complex one which only became [audible] after much study and repeated hearings.[71]

New Instruments, New Sounds

The serialism movement influenced composers who were eager to create the most outrageous avant-garde sound picture possible. In order to do so, they availed themselves of a wide array of devices previously unheard in classical—or any other style—of music. For example, in the 1930s, French composer Edgard Varèse wrote music for Latin percussion instruments, metal chains, anvils, and sirens. In 1958 Varèse created *Poèm électronique,* an extremely influential piece of early electronic music. The work was composed on eleven separate tracks available on a piece of recording tape. Eight minutes in length, *Poèm électronique* is layered with bells,

piano, organ, and various electronically enhanced voices, rhythms, and drums.

Poèm électronique debuted at the 1958 Brussels World's Fair, where repeating tape loops were played at different times over 425 loudspeakers. This created not a single song but an ambience, or mood, for the total environment of the fair. The music, heard by more than 2 million people, was accompanied by a series of flashing colored lights, possibly the first light show. Prendergast describes the importance of the work:

> By demanding twentieth-century instruments for a twentieth-century sound, Varèse was practically applying Debussy's dream of a new music. In his writings Varèse precisely predicted the rise of synthesizers

Edgard Varèse, in his New York City studio in 1955, makes music by thumping on tubes. Varèse used a variety of unusual instruments.

Stockhausen's Space Music

Music journalist Mark Prendergast describes the music of Karlheinz Stockhausen in the 1970s:

At the height of his fame Stockhausen would be the star of the World Fair of 1970 held at Osaka. Inside West Germany's spherical metallic-blue pavilion, dotted with points of light, an instrumental ensemble augmented by electronics would perform over a nine month period all of the works Stockhausen had written up to then. For five and a half hours each day the composer would balance and control the sound from a large mixing console via fifty-five loudspeakers arranged in seven rings. A total of one million listeners were attracted to this futuristic scenario, reminiscent of "musical space travel" . . . .

[In 1977 Stockhausen devoted] himself to the creation of an enormous opera cycle, *Licht* (*Light*), for solo voices, solo instruments, solo dancers, choirs, orchestras, ballet, electronic sound and concrete music. This massive concept, encompassing the history of the [universe] based on the [importance] of the seven days of the week in various cultures, was Stockhausen's attempt to outdo Wagner by creating the longest "total-art piece" . . . in the history of music. Each "day" would have its own opera lasting several hours, and each opera would take three and a half years to execute, with various parts staged around Europe.

Mark Prendergast. *The Ambient Century*. New York: Bloomsbury, 2000, p. 55.

and the role of sampling equipment in creating new sounds. . . . What is striking is that his ideas for light and color projection, his use of . . . the sound environment of *Poèm électronique* were a blueprint for Ambient Techno Music of the 1990s.[72]

During the 1950s, Varèse was joined by a wide array of composers interested in using electronic instruments in serial, ambient, and experimental music. German composer Karlheinz Stockhausen, an alumnus of the Darmstadt gatherings, was the leading composer of the avant-garde. Stockhausen was a talented jazz musician who could play oboe, violin, and piano. Beginning in 1952, Stockhausen

Karlheinz Stockhausen tries out a musical instrument he made out of aluminum plates in 1974. Stockhausen is known for his interest in using various sounds for his compositions.

played *musique concrete,* or *concrete music,* a style that involved recording various sounds on tape, then cutting and splicing the tape at various angles to produce different attacks and tapering off of sound. This technique often produced a pleasing random kaleidoscopic sound.

In addition to his musique concrete, Stockhausen was a studio wizard who generated a wide variety of sounds using electronic means. When he traveled to the United States to lecture at UCLA in 1966, he met with the Grateful Dead and Jefferson Airplane, bands which pioneered the psychedelic San Francisco sound based on improvisation and distorted electric guitars. Stockhausen also worked with John Lennon of the Beatles, and his musique concrete technique can be heard in the Beatles' songs "Revolution 9," "Strawberry Fields Forever," and "Being for the Benefit of Mr. Kite."

The Sounds of Silence

Experimental composer John Cage places coins and screws between the strings of a piano in 1949 to create alternate tunings. Cage manipulated instruments in unusual ways to create his minimalist sound.

Stockhausen spent the 1970s performing electronically generated avant-garde music that sounded like it was from outer space. Meanwhile, U.S. composer John Cage took his inspiration from minimalism.

The minimalist movement was based on the motto "less is more,"[73] coined by German-American architect Ludwig Mies van der Rohe. Minimalist composers stripped classical music down to its most basic elements, continuously repeating several melodic and rhythm patterns with slight alteration in tempo and timbre. Cage was also influenced by the Zen Buddhist belief that the highest purpose is to have no purpose. The end result of these concepts was the 1952 piece "4'33"," a work of silence that lasted four minutes, thirty-three seconds in which the ambient sound of the concert hall—people shifting in their seats, coughing, shuffling their feet, and whispering to one another— was intended to be the evening's music.

Cage was proud of his ability to push artistic boundaries and sabotage conventional notions of music, even if it meant annoying the audience. As the composer once said, "If my work is accepted I must move on to the point where it isn't."[74] While Cage's work was controversial, many did come to accept his music. By the time of his death in 1992, Cage was seen as one of the twentieth century's most influential composers. Rock acts including Frank Zappa, Sonic Youth, and Stereolab all acknowledge a debt to Cage.

A Song Played for 639 Years

After avant-garde composer John Cage died in 1992, interest in his work remained high. In 2001 German organizers decided to play Cage's composition "As Slow As Possible" (ASLSP) for 639 years, as the following article from BBC World Service explains:

Last week, The John Cage Project launched what they claim will be the world's longest musical recital. Organ2/ASLSP is due to be performed on the town organ in Halberstadt in northern Germany over a decidedly leisurely 639 years. Apparently some 360 spectators, paid [about $15] to see the recital's organist inflate his instrument's bellows and they'll have to come back in another 18 month's time in order to hear him play the first chord—and one each year or so thereafter. Providing that sponsors can be found, the performance is scheduled to reach its finale in 2640, with a half time interval planned in 2319. Although Cage originally wrote ASLSP in 1992 as a 20-minute piece for piano, for many years musicologists have deliberated over just how slow, as slow as possible really is. Whilst purists have argued that time is infinite, the John Cage Organ Foundation agreed on the figure of 639 years to correspond with the number of years since the construction of Germany's first block single organ.

BBC World Service. "A Time for John Cage: Arts and Entertainment." September 11, 2001. http://www.bbc.co.uk.

Destiny's Orders

From Mahler to Stockhausen, composers of the modern era endeavored to create atmospheres, sonic spaces, and ambience. Inspired by the blares, whistles, rumbles, and screeches of modern society, few tried to compose songs that listeners could hum along to. Old rules were discarded, and every aspect of classical music was open to radical experimentation.

While audiences were often shocked, rather than soothed, most composers sensed that their sounds would be accepted someday. As Schoenberg eloquently wrote four years before his death in 1951, "I am quite conscious of the fact that a full understanding of my works cannot be expected before some decades. The minds of the musicians, and the audiences, have to mature where they can comprehend my music. I know this . . . and I know that . . . it is my historic duty to write what my destiny orders me to write."[75]

For expressionist, avant-garde, and minimalist composers, the drive to create new music took precedence over the public's need to understand it. As a result, their music changed expectations and had a lasting impact on generations of musicians who followed.

CHAPTER 6

Classical Music in the New Millennium

On January 31, 2012, the Bruckner Orchester Linz debuted Symphony No. 9 by Philip Glass at Carnegie Hall in New York City. Ninth symphonies are a cause of wonder and dread among composers—Beethoven, Schubert, and Mahler all died after composing their legendary ninths. Glass was somewhat nervous about what composers call the "Curse of the Ninth,"[76] but his three-movement piece did not herald his death. After receiving widespread critical acclaim, a recording of Glass's fifty-two-minute Ninth was made available for downloading from the iTunes Store. The symphony, which features music ranging from the somber to the tumultuous, quickly peaked at number fifteen on the iTunes Top 100 Albums chart. This placed Glass's classical masterpiece alongside top-selling albums by the pop singer Adele, the blues rock band Black Keys, and the electronic dance jams of the DJ Skrillex. According to music critic Greg Cahill, the popularity of Glass's Symphony No. 9 proved that classical music sales were healthy in 2012:

> Glass on iTunes reinforces a series of surveys funded by the National Endowment for the Arts that have shown that . . . the number of people listening to classical music in their cars, on mobile devices, and at home, is up. Between 2006 and 2009, classical music accounted for

Composer Philip Glass sits at a piano in 1986. His musical style has been described as polystylism.

only three to four percent of total sales of music in [retail] stores, but on iTunes it was 12 percent of sales.[77]

Many Styles of Music

Glass's foray into digital sales was another step in a long career playing what is known as contemporary classical music. This style, which followed modernism, emerged in the mid-1970s. Those who play contemporary classical music often engage in what is called *polystylism*. Poly means "many," and polystylistic composers combine many different styles of music. They create classical works that draw from jazz, rock, electronic, and even hip-hop music. In recent decades polystylistic composers have come to incorporate modern digital tools into their music, utilizing computers to alter and manipulate sounds.

Glass was an early proponent of polystylism. After starting his career performing minimalist and twelve-tone pieces in New York art museums in the late 1960s, he went on to write symphonies. He also composed several popular operas including *Einstein on the Beach*, and scored music for more than forty movies, including *Naqoyqatsi*, *Kundun*, and *The Truman Show*.

In the 1980s, Glass expanded his audience by collaborating with top-selling rock musicians such as Paul Simon,

The Impact of Philip Glass

In 2012, the work of Philip Glass was described on the composer's website:

> Through his operas, his symphonies, his compositions for his own ensemble . . . Philip Glass has had an extraordinary and unprecedented impact upon the musical and intellectual life of his times. The operas— "Einstein on the Beach," "Satyagraha," "Akhnaten," and "The Voyage," among many others—play throughout the world's leading houses, and rarely to an empty seat. Glass has written music for experimental theater and for Academy Award-winning motion pictures. . . . Indeed, Glass is the first composer to win a wide, multi-generational audience in the opera house, the concert hall, the dance world, in film and in popular music—simultaneously. . . .
>
> There has been nothing "minimalist" about his output. [Since the 1980s] Glass has composed more than twenty operas, large and small; eight symphonies (with others already on the way); two piano concertos and concertos for violin, piano, timpani, and saxophone quartet and orchestra; soundtracks to films . . . string quartets; a growing body of work for solo piano and organ. . . . He presents lectures, workshops, and solo keyboard performances around the world, and continues to appear regularly with the Philip Glass Ensemble.

"Philip Glass Biography." Philip Glass, 2012. www.philipglass.com/bio.php.

Mick Jagger, Leonard Cohen, and David Byrne. During the 1990s, Glass scored symphonies based on two rock albums: *Low* and *Heroes*, originally recorded by rockers David Bowie and Brian Eno. Glass also worked in other musical genres including ambient, electronic, and world music.

The Twenty-First Century Debussy

Like Glass, the British composer Julian Anderson successfully combined several styles of music into critically acclaimed contemporary classical music. Anderson, born in 1967, composed his first score, *Diptych* in 1990 at the age of twenty-three. This first composition, along with several related pieces—including *Sea Drift* and *Khorovod*—had common polystylistic elements. They incorporated traditional folk music from Scotland, Ireland, and Eastern Europe.

Anderson's use of polystylism also included the clever utilization of digital instruments. In his 2004 composition

British composer Julian Anderson includes the use of digital instruments in his musical compositions.

Book of Hours, the composer required nineteen players and "live electronics,"[78] which included a keyboard synthesizer, two computers, six loudspeakers, and a mixing console typically used in a recording studio to adjust sound levels and tones. The electronics added tone color and rhythms throughout the piece. Samples, or pre-recorded sounds, were used to recreate the sound of scratchy old vinyl records like those the composer heard during his childhood.

In 2012 Anderson debuted his orchestral work *The Discovery of Heaven* based on a book by Harry Mulisch in which two men embark on a mystical journey. *The Discovery of Heaven* incorporates several largely unheard musical styles including Slavic folk music and Japanese Gagaku, or court music, which dates from the ninth century. Music reviewer Andrew Clark offered high praise for *The Discovery of Heaven* and its composer, "the score sounds like the work of a 21st-century Debussy in its precise yet shimmering array of color, timbre, and gesture."[79]

Rouse's Rage

While Anderson found arrays of color in ancient folk music, U.S. composer Christopher Rouse takes inspiration from the pounding rhythms of rock. As music critic Barrymore Laurence Scherer explains, "Rouse's music often exhibits an alluring tension between the steady influence of Classical and Romantic European tradition and his own penchant for the violent, driving expressions of Led Zeppelin and other rock bands."[80] Rouse's love of Led Zeppelin was expressed in the composition "Bonham," named after the group's drummer John Bonham who died in 1980. Critic David S. Gutman describes the work: "There's a rock drummer at the heart of this piece, and he is both the foundation and motivation for a series of wave-like crescendos which shake, rattle and roll their way out of tense, simmering patterns, ever ready to come to the boil."[81]

Incorporating hard rock rhythms into classical music might be enough for some composers, but Rouse found beats even more ferocious than those of Led Zeppelin. The song "Ogoun Badagris," from Rouse's 2000 album *Passion*

Wheels, was inspired by drumming heard during voodoo rituals in Haiti. According to Rouse, "Ogoun Badagris is one of the most terrible and violent of all Voodoo *loas* (deities) and he can be appeased only by human blood sacrifice. This work may thus be interpreted as a dance of appeasement."[82]

"Ogoun Badagris" is not only frightening to listen to, but it is a rare piece for symphony drummers. The song calls for performers to pound on metal plates and conga drums and shake out rhythms on sleigh bells and giant rattles. Few other orchestral pieces allow percussionists to perform in such an unrestrained manner.

Passion Wheels also features the song "Ku-Ka-Ilimoku," inspired by Ku, the Hawaiian god of war. Few, if any, composers have ever written such a wild, rhythmical piece meant to be performed on Hawaiian war drums. As Rouse explains, "this work for percussion ensemble is best viewed as a savage, propulsive war dance."[83] Rouse's fierce compositions are not limited to percussion ensembles. He called his String Quartet No. 1, from the 2009 album *Transfiguration,* harsh and brutal, containing "17 minutes of rage."[84]

Humor and Love

While Rouse often alarmed listeners, he could also exhibit humor by incorporating pop music into his work. The 2003 composition "The Nevill Feast" is built on a repeating rock-like chord pattern and features instrumentation commonly found in rock-and-roll bands. These include an electric bass and percussion instruments such as maracas, a drum set, bongos, and a cowbell. At one point during "The Nevill Feast," an orchestra member blows a police whistle, which can provoke peals of laughter in the audience.

Perhaps Rouse's most unusual composition, "Odna Zhizn" (A Life), is based on a musical experiment. Rouse devised a system that translated the letters of the alphabet into twenty-six musical pitches. In this 2008 orchestral work, Rouse describes events that occurred in the life of his girlfriend, using the notes to spell out various words, phrases, and names. As Rouse describes the piece, "it was an enormous challenge for me to fashion these materials into what I hoped would be a satisfying musical experience that functions both as the public portrayal of an extraordinary life as well as a private love letter."[85]

Judith Weir's Contemporary Operas

Like Julian Anderson, Scottish composer Judith Weir found great inspiration in folk music styles. Born in 1954, Weir began her career in the mid-1970s. Her early pieces were influenced by the traditional regional songs of China, Spain, and Serbia. Her piece *Airs from Another Planet* goes beyond worldly folk music. Displaying her off-kilter sense of humor, Weir gave the work the subtitle "traditional music from outer space."[86]

Weir had comical intentions when she composed *King Harald's Saga* in 1979. The historical opera tells the epic story of Norwegian king Harald Hadradi's failed invasion of England in 1066. Rather than stage the opera with a cast of hundreds, Weir wrote it for a solo soprano who sings all eight parts. The entire opera lasts around ten minutes. Weir says that in writing the piece, "a certain amount of compression [was] necessary."[87]

Weir went on to write several more well-regarded operas. Her 1990 *The Vanishing Bridegroom* is a supernatural tale that draws from Scottish folksongs. Weir's 1994 opera *Blond Eckbert* is taken from a dark, supernatural tale written in 1797 by the German romantic author Ludwig Tieck. The opera features a magic bird whose singing reflects the changing moods of the characters throughout the opera.

Television Opera

Weir's 2005 opera *Armida* is perhaps her most ambitious. Rather than stage the opera at a symphony hall, Weir had *Armida* filmed for television. The story is loosely based on the epic poem *Jerusalem Delivered*, written in 1581 by the Italian poet Torquato Tasso.

Jerusalem Delivered takes place during the First Crusade, in which eleventh-century Christian knights invaded

Judith Weir's *Miss Fortune*

The 2011 opera *Miss Fortune* is based on a simple Sicilian fable that was transformed by composer Judith Weir into a parable about modern life. *Miss Fortune* follows the life of Tina Fortune, whose wealthy parents lose all their money in a stock market crash. Miss Fortune is forced to take a series of menial jobs at a clothing factory, a food wagon, and a laundry mat. Eventually Tina confronts a supernatural being, Fate, and she makes a deal. Fate allows Tina to win the lottery, find a boyfriend, and live happily ever after.

While the tale of *Miss Fortune* is simple, the production was staged with high-tech settings and scenery more commonly found at rock concerts. The stage flashed with laser lights, light-emitting diode (LED) sculptures, abstract animation, and manipulated movie footage. A giant movable polygon sculpture, about 40 by 23 feet (12 by 7 meters) in size, occupied different positions throughout the production. The sculpture acted as a screen for video and lights while towering over the cast and stage. With its dark presence, the polygon was nearly as important as the opera's cast. Weir meant it to serve as a symbol of the insignificance of human existence when faced with the power of Fate.

Jerusalem and battled with Muslim defenders who controlled the city. In Tasso's poem, a witch named Armida enters the Christian camp with the intention of killing the great knight, Rinaldo with a magic spell. Instead Armida falls in love with Rinaldo and takes him away to a magical island. Rinaldo soon leaves Armida heartbroken.

In Weir's reimagining of *Jerusalem Delivered*, Tasso's knight Rinaldo appears as a British army officer. He is fighting in Iraq after the country was invaded by the United States and Great Britain in 2003. Weir's Rinaldo is a peace-loving man who is troubled by his role in the Iraq War.

The supernatural Armida is recast by Weir as a famous television reporter in the mold of the CNN correspondent Christiane Amanpour. Weir's Armida is also conflicted. She is against the Iraq War but loves her role as a TV journalist. Armida enters the British army camp to interview soldiers and falls in love with Rinaldo. Instead of traveling to a mag-

Judith Weir's opera Miss Fortune *is performed at Austria's Bregenz Festival in 2011. The opera blends traditional tales with contemporary themes and uses elaborate sets including a giant movable sculpture for video projections.*

ical island, Armida transports Rinaldo in a news helicopter to a beautiful city in Morocco. The two lovers give up their careers to grow flowers while Armida's fictional news channel stops covering wars and focuses instead on gardening shows.

Weir commented on *Armida* when it was being filmed for BBB Channel 4: "I wanted to write an opera which deals in part with the TV coverage of wars. . . . I find the story interesting because it's both a love story and a political story. But it's a love story, too, about the affair between the media and the war operation. It's also a war story about love—because love can be a war as well."[88]

In 2011 Weir continued to blend traditional tales with contemporary themes. Her opera *Miss Fortune*—about a modern woman faced with financial difficulties—is based on the Sicilian folktale, "Sfortuna," a story about the whims of fate.

The Sacred Space of Tansy Davies

Weir was among a growing number of female composers receiving media attention in the twenty-first century. Some, like Tansy Davies, brought entirely new musical sensibilities to an ancient art. Davies was born in London in 1973 and began her musical career as a teenager singing and playing guitar in a rock band. She wrote her first classical composition at the age of twenty-two, and the piece won the BBC Young Composer's Competition of 1996. Davies went on to write works that were performed by the world's most respected orchestras including the London Symphony and the BBC Scottish Symphony.

Davies was drawn to the mystical and supernatural. In her 2004 work *Iris,* the saxophone solo is meant to bring forth images of a shaman, a healer whose spirit travels through both the physical and supernatural worlds. Davies continued to evoke otherworldly sounds in her 2010 requiem *As With Voices and With Tears.* The piece was performed by a youth choir that sings a haunting melody as a string orchestra plays slightly off-key notes. Digital samples provide sounds such as bells, birdsongs, and footsteps. *As With Voices and With Tears* was based on a moving poem of the same name written by nineteenth-century American poet Walt Whitman. It is about a father and son killed together in combat. To translate Whitman's words into music, Davies utilized the technique perfected by Rouse, as music critic Stephen Prichard explains:

> Davies extracted her music from this moving text using a system that assigned a different pitch to each letter of the alphabet, further molding or sculpting the notes and enriching the harmonies into tonal clusters, so that the vocal lines are often only a semitone apart—difficult to sing but both arresting and mysterious in effect.[89]

Not all of Davies's compositions are as somber as her Whitman piece. Inspired by classic rock, alternative rock, funk, jazz, and avant-garde, her music can throb, bubble, jangle, and pound. The sound thrives on abrupt collisions between pop and classical elements. This is reflected in the unusual and insightful directions she includes with her scores, advising musicians to play pieces variously as "urban, muscular," "seedy, low slung," "stealthy," and "solid, grinding."[90]

In the orchestra piece *Grind Show*, Davies demonstrated her ability to write urban, seedy, and grinding music. She contrasts typical classical solos for violin, flute, and piano with clanking digital samples and the gritty funk sound of a bass clarinet. Reviewer Paul Griffiths describes the feelings and images evoked by the music:

> Listening to it is a bit like being on a train that can bump suddenly from racing velocity to slowness, and that can somehow rattle along in a somewhat dislocated fashion at several different speeds at the same time. Meanwhile, the view out of the window will be changing. You may think you see a city crossroads at night—people rushing, people still, warm air thumping from a club doorway, the gleam of a streetlamp on the [fender] of a car. But blink and the scene shifts. It's a medieval landscape, maybe retouched in fluorescent colors. Or, as the station turns to Bach, it's Baroque. Or it's a sacred space, eastern or western, ancient or modern, with chant rising.[91]

Bach to Techno

Davies often debuted her pieces at London's trendiest dance clubs, where she delivered classical music to new generations of fans. In doing so, Davies proved there was an audience for classical music that was youthful, accessible, and ready for some humor. Her innovative music, like that of Weir, Rouse, and Glass, shows that the music of the Western world has changed considerably over the past one hundred years. Chants reminiscent of those played in the thirteenth century are heard on television commercials, and fifteenth-century madrigals are regularly played at annual Renaissance Festivals.

The musical styles of Bach, Mozart, and Beethoven have been deconstructed, rebuilt, and even blended with jazz, rock and roll, and techno music. Orchestras from Africa to India and China continue to perform classical music once confined to only Europe, Canada, and the United States.

The Congo's Symphony Orchestra

In the twenty-first century few things have better demonstrated the broad reach of classical music than the existence of the Kimbanguist Symphony Orchestra. The orchestra is based in Kinshasa, the capital city of the war-torn Democratic Republic of the Congo, the poorest country in the world. The players in the orchestra faced incredible hardships and, like most other citizens in the Congo, lived on less than $50 a month.

In 2012 the Kimbanguist Symphony consisted of two hundred instrumentalists and singers. They were brought together by an ex-airline pilot named Armand Diangienda who taught himself to read music and play piano, trombone, guitar, and cello in the early 1990s. Diangienda convinced people from his local church to form an orchestra and soon they were learning to play on donated instruments and those rescued from local thrift shops. After several years of practice, the Kimbanguist Symphony Orchestra was skillfully playing music first conceived in eighteenth-century Austria. In 2012, the orchestra was featured on the TV show *60 Minutes*. Reporter Bob Simon was overwhelmed by the orchestra's beautiful rendition of Beethoven's Ninth: "Beethoven came alive. It's called the Ode to Joy, the last movement of Beethoven's last symphony. It has been played with more expertise before . . . . but with more joy? Hard to imagine."

Bob Simon. "Joy in the Congo: A Musical Miracle." *60 Minutes*, April 8, 2012. www.cbsnews.com.

The Kimbanguist Symphony Orchestra plays a piece by Mozart in Kinshasa, Congo, in 2006.

In an era when the ring of a cell phone can play the opening notes of Beethoven's Fifth, the musically impossible has become commonplace. Western music, which once followed strict rules overseen by the church and princes, has been opened to experimentation by a new generation of composers raised on the Beatles, Prince, and Kanye West. Where music was once confined to the palace, the church, or the exclusive concert hall, it can now be heard in movie theaters, automobiles, and on MP3 players. Classical music, once heard only by a select few, has come to be loved by millions of people around the world.

NOTES

Introduction: When All Music Was Classical

1. Stanley Sadie and Alison Latham, eds. *The Cambridge Music Guide.* Cambridge, England: Cambridge University Press, 2000, p. 21.
2. Robert Sherman and Philip Seldon. *The Complete Idiot's Guide to Classical Music.* New York: Alpha, 1997, p. 6.

Chapter 1: Medieval and Renaissance Roots

3. William Mann. *James Galway's Music in Time.* New York: Henry N. Abrams, 1982, p. 14.
4. Donald Jay Grout. *A History of Western Music.* New York: W.W. Norton, 1973, pp. 11–12.
5. Dhun H. Sethna. *Classical Music for Everybody.* Sierra Madre, CA: Fitzwilliam, 1997, p. 43.
6. Grout. *A History of Western Music,* pp. 21–22.
7. Grout. *A History of Western Music,* p. 62.
8. Grout. *A History of Western Music,* p. 76.
9. Mann. *James Galway's Music in Time,* pp. 94–95.
10. Will Durant. *The Renaissance.* New York: Simon & Schuster, 1953, p. 599.
11. Alec Harman. *Man and His Music Part 1: Mediaeval and Early Renaissance Music.* London: Barrie & Jenkins, 1988, p. 205.
12. Mann. *James Galway's Music in Time,* p. 51.
13. Quoted in Sadie and Latham. *The Cambridge Music Guide,* p. 135.

Chapter 2: The Baroque Era

14. Quoted in George J. Buelow, ed. *The Late Baroque Era.* Englewood Cliffs, NJ: Prentice Hall, 1994, p. 1.
15. Quoted in Buelow. *The Late Baroque Era,* p. 1.
16. David Ewen. *Opera.* New York: Franklin Watts, 1972, p. 7.
17. Quoted in David Ewen. *Opera,* p. 9.
18. David Ewen. *Opera,* p. 10.
19. David Ewen. *Opera,* p. 13.
20. Sadie and Latham. *The Cambridge Music Guide,* p. 147.
21. Buelow. *The Late Baroque Era,* p. 6.
22. Sherman and Seldon. *The Complete Idiot's Guide to Classical Music,* p. 156.
23. Quoted in Charles Sanford Terry.

Johann Sebastian Bach. London: Oxford University Press, 1972, p. 70.

24. Albert Schweitzer. *J.S. Bach, vol. 1.* New York: Dover, 1966, p. 407.

25. Quoted in Sherman and Seldon. *The Complete Idiot's Guide to Classical Music*, p. 159.

26. Sherman and Seldon. *The Complete Idiot's Guide to Classical Music*, p. 161.

Chapter 3: The Classical Period

27. Quoted in Charles Rosen. *The Classical Style.* W.W. Norton, 1997, p. 19.

28. Sherman and Seldon. *The Complete Idiot's Guide to Classical Music*, p. 155.

29. Sadie and Latham. *The Cambridge Music Guide*, p. 220.

30. Sherman and Seldon. *The Complete Idiot's Guide to Classical Music*, pp. 76–77.

31. A. Peter Brown. *The Symphonic Repertoire, vol. 2: The First Golden Age of the Viennese Symphony: Haydn, Mozart, Beethoven, and Schubert.* Bloomington: University of Indiana Press, 2002, p. 301.

32. Quoted in Neal Zaslaw, ed. *The Classical Era.* Englewood Cliffs, NJ: Prentice Hall, 1989, p. 268.

33. Mann. *James Galway's Music in Time*, p. 144.

34. Quoted in Sherman and Seldon. *The Complete Idiot's Guide to Classical Music*, p. 170.

35. Quoted in Zaslaw. *The Classical Era*, p. 290.

36. Quoted in James Webster and Georg Feder. *The New Grove Haydn.* Palgrave, NY: Macmillan, 2002, p. 28.

37. Quoted in Alfred Einstein. *Mozart: His Character, His Work.* New York: Oxford University Press, 1945.

38. Quoted in Hans Gal, ed. *The Musician's World.* New York: Arco, 1965, p. 70.

39. Harold C. Schonberg. *The Lives of the Great Composers.* New York: W.W. Norton, 1981, p. 94.

40. Schonberg. *The Lives of the Great Composers*, p. 109.

41. Quoted in Rosen. *The Classical Style*, p. 19.

42. Franz Wegeler and Ferdinand Ries. *Beethoven Remembered.* Arlington, VA: Great Oceans, 1987, p. 88.

43. Mann. *James Galway's Music in Time*, p. 162.

44. Sherman and Seldon. *The Complete Idiot's Guide to Classical Music*, p. 177.

45. Quoted in Alexander Thayer. *The Life of Ludwig van Beethoven, vol 3.* Ann Arbor, MI: UMI, 1989, p. 300.

Chapter 4: The Romantic Era

46. Quoted in Harvey Sachs. *The Ninth: Beethoven and the World in 1824.* New York: Random House, 2010, p. 10.

47. Sherman and Seldon. *The Complete*

Idiot's Guide to Classical Music, p. 187.

48. Marion Bauer and Ethel Peyser. *Music Through the Ages.* New York: G.P. Putnam's Sons, 1967, p. 412.
49. Donald J. Grout and Claude V. Palisca. *A History of Western Music*, 4th ed. New York: W.W. Norton, 1988, p. 686.
50. Quoted in Sherman and Seldon. *The Complete Idiot's Guide to Classical Music*, p. 193.
51. Harold C. Schonberg. *The Lives of the Great Composers*, p. 181.
52. Quoted in Grout and Palisca. *A History of Western Music*, p. 709.
53. David Pogue and Scott Speck. *Classical Music for Dummies.* Chicago, IL: IDG, 1997, p. 55.
54. Bauer and Peyser. *Music Through the Ages*, p. 469.
55. Quoted in Schonberg. *The Lives of the Great Composers*, p. 256.
56. Bauer and Peyser. *Music Through the Ages*, p. 493.
57. Sadie and Latham. *The Cambridge Music Guide*, p. 352.
58. Sadie and Latham. *The Cambridge Music Guide*, p. 345.

Chapter 5: The Musical Art of the Modern Era

59. Mark Prendergast. *The Ambient Century.* New York: Bloomsbury, 2000, p. 11.
60. Quoted in Sherman and Seldon. *The Complete Idiot's Guide to Classical Music*, p. 212.
61. Pogue and Speck. *Classical Music for Dummies*, p. 60.
62. Quoted in Sadie and Latham. *The Cambridge Music Guide*, p. 394.
63. Bauer and Peyser. *Music Through the Ages*, p. 567.
64. Mann. *James Galway's Music in Time*, p. 300.
65. Quoted in Edward A. Lippman. Musical Aesthetics: *The Twentieth Century*. Hillsdale, NY: Pendragon, p. 160.
66. Grout and Palisca. *A History of Western Music*, 4th ed., p. 849.
67. Sherman and Seldon. *The Complete Idiot's Guide to Classical Music*, p. 217.
68. Sherman and Seldon. *The Complete Idiot's Guide to Classical Music*, p. 218.
69. Grout and Palisca. *A History of Western Music*, 4th ed., p. 859.
70. Grout and Palisca. *A History of Western Music*, 4th ed., p. 865.
71. Grout and Palisca. *A History of Western Music*, 4th ed., p. 866.
72. Prendergast. *The Ambient Century*, p. 36
73. Quoted in Curt Cloninger. *Fresher Styles for Web Designers: More Eye Candy from the Underground.* Berkeley: New Riders, 2009, p. 72.
74. Quoted in BBC World Service. "A Time for John Cage: Arts and Entertainment," September 11, 2001. www.bbc.co.uk/worldservice/arts/highlights/010911_cage.shtml.
75. Quoted in Harold C. Schonberg. *The Lives of the Great Composers*, p. 602.

Chapter 6: Classical Music in the New Millennium

76. Quoted in James C. Taylor. "Philip Glass, 75, Has an iTunes Hit with His Ninth Symphony." *Los Angeles Times*, February 2, 2012. http://latimesblogs.latimes.com/culturemonster/2012/02/philip-glass-75-has-an-itunes-hit-with-his-ninth-symphony.html.

77. Greg Cahill. "Philip Glass–Top of the Pops. Wow!" *All Things Strings*, February 13, 2012. www.allthingsstrings.com/News/News/Philip-Glass-Top-of-the-Pops.-Wow.

78. Julian Anderson. "Book of Hours." Faber Music, 2012. www.fabermusic.comRepertoire-Details.aspx?ID=4257.

79. Quoted in "Julian Anderson—'A 21st-Century Debussy.'" Faber Music, 2012. www.fabermusic.com/news/story/julian-anderson-%E2%80%93-%E2%80%98a-21st-century-debussy%E2%80%99.aspx?ComposerId=13.

80. Barrymore Laurence Scherer. *A History of American Classical Music.* Naperville, IL: SourceBooks Mediafusion, 2007, p. 216.

81. Quoted in "Bonham." Christopher Rouse, 2012. www.christopherrouse.com/bonhampress.html.

82. "Ogoun Badagris." Christopher Rouse, May 24, 2012. www.christopherrouse.com/ogounpress.html.

83. "Ku-Ka-Ilimoku." Christopher Rouse, 2012. www.christopherrouse.com/kukapress.html.

84. Quoted in Doyle Armbrust. "Calder Quartet." Alliance Artist Management, 2012. www.allianceartistmanagement.com/artist.php?id=calderquartet&aview=acclaim&nid=3285.

85. "Odna Zhizn." Christopher Rouse, 2012. www.christopherrouse.com/odnazhiznpress.html.

86. Quoted in "Judith Weir." LA Phil, 2012. www.laphil.com/philpedia/judith-weir.

87. Quoted in Tom Service. "A Guide to Judith Weir's Music." *The Guardian*, May 28, 2012. www.guardian.co.uk/music/tomserviceblog/2012/may/28/judith-weir-contemporary-composers-guide.

88. Quoted in Stuart Jeffries. "Desert Bloom." *The Guardian*, November 30, 2005. www.guardian.co.uk/film/2005/dec/01/classicalmusicandopera.

89. Quoted in "South Bank Sky Arts Award." Tansy Davies, 2012. www.tansydavies.com.

90. Quoted in "Davies, Tansy." *Re:New Music*, 2012. http://renewmusic.org/composers/davies-tansy.

91. Paul Griffiths. "Hold Tight." Tansy Davies, 2012. www.tansydavies.com.

Claudio Abbado

Alban Berg Collection, 2004

Academy of Ancient Music, Emma Kirkby, Carolyn Watkinson, et al.

Handel-Messiah, 1991

Handel frequently updated his famed *Messiah*—changing some parts and adding others. The Academy of Ancient Music recreates a specific performance from a score written by Handel in April 1754. This recording is considered one of the finest versions of Handel's definitive work.

Academy of St. Martin in the Fields and Sir Neville Marriner

Brandenburg Concertos/Orchestral Suites, 2002

On this CD collection, some of the world's greatest musicians, led by renowned conductor Neville Marriner, perform Bach's most famous compositions.

BBC Symphony Orchestra and the London Sinfonietta

Anderson: Alhambra Fantasy; Khorovod; The Stations of the Sun, 2006

This album demonstrates why English composer Julian Anderson has been called the twenty-first-century Debussy. With its glittering colors, timbres, and textures, these pieces feature folk dance melodies, stunning percussion, and joyous brass works.

Jozef de Beenhouwer

Clara Schumann: Complete Piano Works, 2001

Benedictine Monks of Santo Domingo de Silos

Chant, 1994

Although Gregorian chants fell out of favor by the thirteenth century, they became incredibly popular in the 1990s. This 1994 album, featuring songs that were eight hundred years old, sold more than 5 million copies within a year.

Berlin Philharmonic Orchestra (Berliner Philharmoniker)

Hector Berlioz: Symphonie Fantastique; Dance of the Sylphs; Dance of the Will-o'-the-Wisps, 1990

Mozart: The Magic Flute, 2010

This magical opera features *singspiel*, a popular eighteenth-century form that includes both singing and spoken dialogue. Since its premiere in 1791, this masterpiece has become one of Mozart's most popular operas and remains in production around the world.

Mozart: The Symphonies, 2006

Schubert: 8 Symphonies, 2001

Webern: Passacaglia / Schoenberg: Variations Op.31/ Berg: 3 Pieces from the "Lyric Suite"; 3 Pieces for Orchestra Op.6, 1999

This CD is a celebration of difficult twelve-tone compositions written by the giants of serialism and played by one of the world's greatest orchestras.

Leonard Bernstein, Collegiate Chorale, New York Philharmonic

Bach: St. Matthew Passion, 1999

Ludwig Böhme and Josquin des Prez Chamber Choir

Josquin des Prez: Missa Pange Lingua, 2011

Boston Symphony Orchestra

Ravel: Boléro, 1991

This ballet, composed by Maurice Ravel in 1928, was one of the first large ensemble pieces to employ saxophones. The piece also makes fine use of bassoons, clarinets, trombones, tubas, and other orchestral instruments.

John Cage

In a Landscape, 1995

Claudio Cavina and Ensemble La Venexiana

Monteverdi: L'Orfeo, 2007

This ensemble showcases the work of the maestro Monteverdi, who created new musical ways to express emotion while laying the foundations for the operatic style that dominated classical music for several centuries.

Chamber Orchestra of the New Dutch Academy

Stamitz/Richter: New Dutch Academy Mannheim Project, 2003

Cleveland Orchestra

Schumann: The Four Symphonies; Manfred Overture, 1996

Tansy Davies

Spine, 2012

Dietrich Fischer-Dieskau and Christoph Eschenbach

Schumann: Lieder, 2008

John Eliot Gardiner and the English Baroque Soloists

Water Music and Music for the Royal Fireworks, 2001

Philip Glass and the Bruckner Orchester Linz

Symphony No. 9, 2012

Glass's Ninth, which debuted at number fifteen on the iTunes Top 100 Albums, is at various points muscular, tumultuous, and somber. With this work, Glass reminds listeners that classical music is as unique and important in the twenty-first century as it was in Mozart's time.

Philip Glass and the Philip Glass Ensemble

KOYAANISQATSI (Complete Original Soundtrack Version), 2009

Christopher Herrick

Bach: Complete Organ Music, 2002

Bach wrote hundreds of sonatas, fugues, concertos, and other pieces for the organ, and renowned British organist Herrick has assembled 362 of those songs for this ambitious compilation.

Hilliard Ensemble

English and Italian Renaissance Madrigals, 2000

Walter Kraft

Buxtehude: Complete Organ Music, 2004

Bernhard Landauer, Michael Posch, and Ensemble Unicorn

Dufay: Chansons, 1996

Andrew Lawrence-King, Ellen L. Hargis, Hille Perl, and Paul O'Dette

Il Zazzerino: Music of Jacopo Peri, 1999

London Philharmonic Orchestra

Mahler: The Complete Works—150th Anniversary Box, 2010

Everything Mahler ever wrote is presented in this box of sixteen CDs released on the 150th anniversary of the composer's birthday. The music was taken from London Philharmonic performances recorded between 1949 and 2010, with heavy emphasis on the 1960s. The older performances have been remixed and digitized to achieve a clear, modern presentation of Mahler's often emotional masterpieces.

London Philharmonic Orchestra and the London Philharmonic Choir

Handel: The Messiah, 2002

London Symphony Orchestra

Beethoven: The Nine Symphonies, 2006

Bizet: L'Arlésienne Suites Nos. 1 & 2, Carmen Suite, 2007

The Works of Arnold Schoenberg, Vol. 1, 2009

The Metropolitan Opera Chorus and the Metropolitan Opera Orchestra

Wagner: Der Ring Des Nibelungen (The Ring of the Nibelung), 2002

It took fourteen CDs to hold all fifteen hours of Wagner's greatest opera. While hardly a brief introduction to *The Ring*, this version is replete with performances by every Valkyrie, Rhinemaiden, Giant, and Nibelung, as intended by the composer.

Orchestra of the Israeli Opera

Aïda, 2013

Verdi's grand opera was recorded on two high-definition, multitrack surround sound CDs in 2011. US-born soprano Kristin Lewis plays the leading role of the beautiful Aïda.

Orlando Consort and the Vocal Quartet

Philippe de Vitry and the Ars Nova, 2011

This recording of fourteenth-century vocal music is both beautiful and haunting and demonstrates the power of de Vitry, who the poet Petrarch called the greatest philosopher of the age.

Peter Phillips and the Tallis Scholars

The Tallis Scholars: English Madrigals, (plus 7 English Anthems), 2006

Christopher Rouse

Passion Wheels, 2000

The composer's love of passionate rhythms can be heard on "Ku-Ka-Ilimoku" featuring indigenous Hawaiian war drums and "Ogoun Badagris" based on Haitian voodoo rituals. Few composers have tread this ground, and Rouse's orchestrations skill are as sophisticated as his creative inspirations.

Royal Concertgebouw

Varèse: The Complete Works, 1998

Rossini: William Tell, 2006

As the grand finale of Rossini's long and successful career, this four-hour opera about the fifteenth-century Swiss folk hero is preserved on three CDs. The historical recordings, from an exciting live performance in Naples in 1965, have been remastered to deliver a crisp, clear sound.

Franz Schubert

Schubert: Lieder, 1996

Igor Stravinsky

Works of Igor Stravinsky, 2007

While classical music fans can only dream of hearing symphonies conducted by Mozart or Haydn, Stravinsky can be heard conducting his own works on this boxed set with a hefty twenty-two CDs. The remastered works from the 1930s through the late 1960s feature chamber music, choral works, jazz suites, and the composer's greatest hits, including *The Firebird, Oedipus Rex,* and *Rite of Spring.*

Karlheinz Stockhausen

Karlheinz Stockhausen: Gruppen/ Punkte, 2006

Tonus Peregrinus

Léonin and Pérotin: Sacred Music from Notre-Dame Cathedral, 2005

The soaring and magnificent sounds of the twelfth-century polyphonic style continue to resonate centuries after it was invented.

Various Artists

Music of the Second Generation of the Second Viennese School, 1995

The Claude Debussy Collection, 2012

The 99 Most Essential Haydn Masterpieces, 2010

These CDs celebrate the classical style and includes ten symphonies, four piano sonatas, four concertos, and several string quartets and oratorios. Few albums could provide a better education concerning the wide variety of sounds associated with classical music.

The 99 Most Essential Liszt Masterpieces, 2010

This collection features the greatest hits of Liszt and the sounds that created Lisztomania, including *Hungarian Rhapsody, Three Songs From Wilhelm Tell,* and *Four Songs By Victor Hugo.*

The Best of Italian Opera, 1997

Vienna Philharmonic Orchestra

Beethoven: Symphony No. 9, 1995

Recorded in the city where the Ninth premiered, by an orchestra conducted by the maestro Karl Böhm, this is among the slowest version of Beethoven's master work, which allows listeners to appreciate every note.

Antonio Vivaldi

The Four Seasons, 2011

These four beautiful concertos that musically illustrate the seasons required musicians to recreate the sounds of twittering birds, babbling brooks, chattering horse teeth, and pelting hailstorms.

Judith Weir

On Buying a Horse: The Songs of Judith Weir, 2007

With twenty-three short songs, this compellation of Weir's music shows off her folk influences from "Scotch Minstrelsy" to "A Spanish Liederbooklet." Songs from the epic opera *King Harald's Saga* are also included.

Three Operas, 1994

GLOSSARY

a cappella: Solo or group singing performed without instrumental accompaniment.

atonal: Music that lacks a central tone, or key.

counterpoint: When several harmonies are played together it is called counterpoint, or polyphony. Contrapuntal music displays counterpoint.

isorhythm: A musical technique of the ars nova period in the late 1300s that relies on a fixed pattern of notes repeated in a rhythmic pattern.

monophonic: Music that consists of melody only, without accompanying harmony.

oratorio: A grand piece of religious classical music that includes a large orchestra, choir, and soloists.

polyphonic: Music with harmony, that is several complementary notes or melodies sounding at once.

polystylism: The trend of creating music that utilizes multiple styles and composition techniques, blending classical with jazz, rock, electronica, and other musical genres.

timbre: The quality or tone color of a musical instrument or voice.

FOR MORE INFORMATION

Books

Hugh Benham. *Baroque Music in Focus*. London: Rhinegold, 2010. This guide to music and culture in the Baroque era features sections on major genres, suggests complimentary listening and viewing material, and provides in-depth examinations of the lives and careers of Johann Sebastian Bach and George Handel.

Anna Alice Chapin and Richard Wagner. *The Story of the Rhinegold*. London: Nabu, 2010. Originally published in 1897, this book includes Wagner's four music dramas known as *The Ring of the Nibelungs*, complete with the witches, elves, gods, and giants taken from German mythology.

Richard Freedman and Walter Frisch. *Music in the Renaissance*. New York: W.W. Norton, 2012. This book explains how music and other forms of expression were adapted to the changing tastes and ideals during the Renaissance. The authors describe who made music, who sponsored and listened to it, and what social purposes it served.

Darren Henley and Sam Jackson. *Everything You Ever Wanted to Know About Classical Music: But Were Too Afraid to Ask*. London: Elliott & Thompson, 2012. This book makes classical music accessible, simple to understand, and engrossing. Readers can learn musical terms, the history of various genres, and key classical figures over the last thousand years.

Sandra H. Shichtman. *The Joy of Creation: The Story of Clara Schumann*. Greensboro, NC: Morgan Reynolds, 2010. This rich narrative of romantic composer and pianist Clara Schumann is thoroughly researched and provides insight into the complex identity of the accomplished artist.

Websites

BBC Radio 3 Composers (www.bbc.co.uk/radio3/composers). This site hosted by the British Broadcasting Corporation provides a wealth of biographical material about classical composers from John Adams to Alexander Zemlinsky. Podcasts of the informative and entertaining *Composer of the Week* show are also available, along with sound clips and videos of concert performances.

Beethoven Reference Site (www.lv beethoven.co.uk). This site provides detailed information about the life and works of Ludwig van Beethoven, including biographical information, descriptions of places the composer worked and visited, picture galleries, and detailed discussions of each of his concertos, sonatas, and symphonies.

Orpheon Foundation (www.orpheon .org). This Vienna-based foundation provides an online museum of historical stringed instruments from the Renaissance, baroque, and classical periods. The site contains photos, historical information, videos, and recordings featuring about two hundred instruments. Some, like the violin and cello, are familiar, while other, including the violone and baryton, are more obscure.

Philip Glass (www.philipglass.com). This site features news, music, and galleries focusing on the modern era's most prolific composer. Details are provided about dozens of compositions, books, and film scores created by Glass. By clicking the "Glass Engine" link, visitors can navigate through more than sixty of the composer's recorded pieces.

Tansy Davies Composer (www.tansy davies.com). The site of the unique British composer features an MP3 jukebox with selected vocal, solo, chamber, and symphony orchestra works. Visitors to the site can also learn about Davies's works by reading program notes and concert reviews.

Films

Amadeus, 1984

This witty drama about Wolfgang Amadeus Mozart and his musical rival Antonio Salieri provides a rich telling of the great composer's life with lush sets, beautiful costumes, and an Oscar-winning performance.

Beethoven: Eroica, 2003

This well-made British drama recreates a historic moment, June 9, 1804, when Ludwig van Beethoven debuted his masterpiece *Eroica,* or Symphony No. 3, to an audience of aristocrats at the Lobkowitz Palace in Vienna. While there are some historical inaccuracies (for example, Haydn was not in attendance) the orchestral performances are superb.

Beethoven: Symphony No. 9, 1989

This concert film of Beethoven's romantic masterpiece was played by the Czech Philharmonic Orchestra and the Prague Philharmonic Choir not long after Czechoslovakia broke free from the repressive rule of the Soviet Union. Beethoven wrote this symphony as a declaration of universal brotherhood, and this concert's historic significance is complemented by the grandeur of the work.

Handel: Messiah, 2005

This 1982 concert from Westminster Abbey features the Academy of Ancient Music conducted by Christopher Hogwood. The players capture the true baroque sound using instruments in the same style as those of Handel's time. The oboes are all wood (no metal keys), and the trumpets have finger holes (no valves). The soloists, including Emma Kirkby, Judith Nelson, and Carolyn Watkinson, make this performance worth a look.

John Cage: One11 with 103, 1992
Composer John Cage created this unusual film, which consists solely of random, moving shades of light, gray, and black affecting an empty space. The images are accompanied by Cage's orchestral composition "103."

Robert Schumann: A Portrait, 2011
Commemorating the 155th anniversary of Schumann's passing, this film chronicles the composer's life from 1828 to his death in 1856 and features stunning performances by Leonard Bernstein and the Vienna Philharmonic.

Rossini: Il Barbiere di Siviglia (The Barber of Seville), 2010
This production of what is perhaps Rossini's most famous opera, blends humor, drama, and stunning vocal performances by singers of the Metropolitan Opera in New York.

Wagner: Der Ring des Nibelungen, 2012
Staged by producer Robert Lepage and performed by the Metropolitan Opera, this production commemorates the two hundredth anniversary of Wagner's birth. The spectacle, which fills eight DVDs, features a forty-five-ton set of twenty-four planks that form the scenery.

INDEX

PICTURE CREDITS

Cover: bioraven/Shutterstock.com

© Alfredo Dagli Orti/The Art Archive at Art Resource, NY, 58

© AP Images, 76, 78, 89, 91, 103

© AP Images/Schalk van Zvydam, 106

© The Art Archive/Art Resource, NY, 22

© Bettmann/Corbis, 17, 42

© Corbis, 96

© Dea Picture Library/Art Resource, NY, 41

© DeAgostini/Getty Images, 26

© Eileen Tweedy/The Art Archive/Art Resource, NY, 35

© Erich Lessing/Art Resource, NY, 52

© Getty Images, 14, 60, 72, 74, 92

© Hulton-Deutsch Collection/ Corbis, 83

© Imagno/Austrian Archives/Getty Images, 82

Image copyright © The Metropolitan Museum of Art. Image source: Art Resource, NY, 46

© Peter Wilson/Getty Images, 9

© RMN-Grand Palais/Art Resource, NY, 33, 69

© Scala/Art Resource, NY, 20, 54

© Stefano Bianchetti/Corbis, 44

© Steve Pyke/Getty Images, 98

ABOUT THE AUTHOR

Stuart A. Kallen is the author of more than 250 nonfiction books for children and young adults. He has written extensively about science, the environment, music, culture, history, and folklore. In addition, Kallen has written award-winning children's videos and television scripts. In his spare time, he is a singer/songwriter/guitarist who lives in San Diego.